The Elements of Mystery Fiction

The Elements
of
Mystery Fiction

*Writing a
Modern Whodunit*

≈ ≈

by William G. Tapply

Publishers   The Writer, Inc.   Boston

Library of Congress Cataloging-in-Publication Data

Tapply, William G.
    The elements of mystery fiction : writing the modern
whodunit / by William G. Tapply.
    p.   cm.
    ISBN 0-87116-176-1 (pbk.)
    1. Detective and mystery stories—Authorship.   I. Title.
    PN3377.5. D4T36 1995
    808.3'872—dc20   95-596
                                                  CIP

Printed in the United States of America

Contents

Acknowledgments

I AM INDEBTED to all of the people who have directly and indirectly encouraged me and taught me how to be a writer: H. G. Tapply, my father, my first editor, and still one of the best, who showed me how hard it is to make writing look easy; Wilbur Cheever, my high school English teacher, who encouraged me; my college instructors, who insisted that a writer must have something to say; Linda Verigan, who was the first to publish something I wrote and thereby hooked me on it for life; Betsy Rapoport, who bought my first novel and helped me hone my craft thereafter; Jed Mattes, my faithful agent; Otto Penzler, my mystery guru; Nick Lyons, writer, editor, publisher, fly fisherman, friend, and master of all; Rick Boyer, my writing mentor and partner in crime; Sylvia Burack, who continues stubbornly to take the job of editing seriously; my students, who never let me off the hook; my children—Michael, Melissa, and Sarah—who claim to be as proud of me as I am of them; all the mystery writers whose work has entertained, inspired and informed me in my lifetime as a reader; and, Vicki Stiefel, to whom, for a thousand reasons, this book is lovingly dedicated.

THE ELEMENTS OF
MYSTERY FICTION

Introduction

WHEN I BEGAN writing my first mystery novel, I thought I had a crackerjack idea. I had invented characters who intrigued me, I had thought up dramatic scenes and tense conflicts, and I had in mind some vivid settings. I knew where my story would start, I could foresee the direction it would take, and I knew how it would end. I had done enough nonfiction writing to feel confident that I could string the words together. I had even sold a few articles.

I had never tried writing mystery fiction. I had never tried to analyze its elements. So what? Writing is writing, I figured.

That first mystery of mine had everything required of a novel—characters and settings and scenes, themes and plots and subplots, dialogue and description and narrative. When it was finished, it made a gratifyingly tall stack of pages. I was rather proud of my accomplishment. I wasn't ready to say I'd written a book, but I *had* written a book-length manuscript.

It now resides in a cardboard box in the attic, where I lovingly entombed it when I realized that it wasn't very good.

Strangely, I was encouraged by having written a bad novel.

Maybe it's not so strange. The writers I know seem constitutionally unable to allow themselves to be discouraged by failure. Certainly if I *had* been discouraged,

I wouldn't have launched boldly into my second mystery novel. And if I hadn't done that, it never would have been published.

When I started trying to write mystery fiction, I didn't know what I was doing. I'd taken no courses, read no how-to books, belonged to no critique groups.

What I did have were the echoes of hundreds of wonderful books in my head, the deceptively straightforward prose of Dashiell Hammett and Raymond Chandler and Ross Macdonald and the confident narration of Travis McGee and Dr. Watson and Archie Goodwin, and many many others.

Reading good mysteries taught me everything I knew when I began trying to write them. "Read, read, read," said William Faulkner. "Read everything—trash, classics, good and bad, and see how they do it. Just like a carpenter who works as an apprentice and studies the master. Read! You'll absorb it. Then write. If it is good, you'll find out. If it's not, throw it out the window."

I wrote and published several mystery novels without consciously examining the process or analyzing its elements. It was a profound handicap. Instinct often told me when something wasn't right. But ignorance prevented me from figuring it out and fixing it. My editor made me do a lot of revising and rewriting, but even with her guidance, it often felt like trial and error.

Sometimes groups invited me to talk with them about writing. They asked me difficult questions, such as, "Where do you get your ideas?" and "How do you construct your plots?" and "How do you write realistic dialogue?" and "How do you plant clues fairly without being obvious?" They forced me to think about what I was doing.

At first, I stumbled through my answers. But I studied and analyzed the work of other mystery writers and took every opportunity to discuss the craft with them. I read how-to books and magazine articles. And I gradually began to understand the elements of mystery fiction.

This book is my attempt to isolate and analyze those elements, to identify the variables that make the difference between success and failure, and to help you write publishable mystery fiction.

≈ 1 ≈
The Elements of
Mystery Fiction

MYSTERY FICTION was born in 1841 when *Graham's Magazine* published Edgar Allan Poe's short story, "The Murders in the Rue Morgue." Here Poe introduces C. Auguste Dupin, the detective who, through his superior intellect and brilliant powers of observation and deduction, sorts out the clues and identifies the murderer of an old woman and her daughter.

The mystery is a puzzler. Dupin is a genius. When he reveals the culprit, readers gasp in admiration.

Literary murders are as old as the book of Genesis. But no one before Poe, as far as we know, ever wrote a story in which the central plot question was "who did it?" and the hero was a detective who correctly deduced the answer to that question.

If Poe invented mystery fiction, fifty years later Sir Arthur Conan Doyle made it wildly popular. Sherlock Holmes, like Poe's Dupin, is a brilliant detective who gathers clues, ponders them privately, and then fingers the villain in a dramatic scene of revelation near the end of the story. His worshipful roommate and chronicler, Dr. Watson, follows along to report on his friend's activities. Watson is Everyman. He's you, or I, or any reader of average intelligence. Unlike Holmes or his literary predecessor Dupin, Watson is accessible. He speaks directly to readers, who identify with the kindly doctor. He's as baffled by Holmes as readers are, as awed by the detective's deductive powers, as intrigued by his eccentricities.

Conan Doyle, with his down-to-earth narrator, his eccentric genius detective, his sharp portraits of nineteenth-century London, and his mind-bending puzzles, transformed mystery fiction into the stuff of bestsellers, where it has remained ever since.

In the stories of Poe and Doyle and their imitators, mystery readers were not allowed into the minds of literary detectives. Readers had no choice but to remain puzzled while Dupin and Holmes gathered clues and pondered them in private. The reader's reward came when the detective dramatically identified the culprit, explained the villain's method and motive, and enumerated the clues that had led him to his uncanny conclusion.

Agatha Christie converted the mystery into a participatory activity for the reader. Christie introduced the vital and revolutionary element of fair play to mystery fiction, making all the clues that were available to her detective equally available to the reader. Readers who could only watch and marvel at Holmes were invited to look for clues and interpret the behavior of Christie's characters. Readers could match wits with Hercule Poirot or Miss Marple, and when a Christie detective pointed the finger at a murderer, readers could slap their foreheads and say, "Of course! I should have figured that out for myself."

With Christie, mystery reading became a game between writer and reader. "Fool me if you can," begged the reader, "and I'll be disappointed if you don't. I want you to make me admire how cleverly you craft your plot and how well you camouflage your clues. But you'd better play fair."

After Christie, successful mystery yarns did just that. The plots were complex, the puzzles bewildering, the motives obscure, and the murder methods bizarre. The story didn't have to be realistic, nor did the characters need to resemble actual flesh-and-blood people, as long as the clues were laid out fairly—no matter how cleverly they were disguised. The writers of the 1920s and '30s—Dorothy L. Sayers, S. S. Van Dine, Ellery Queen, Erle Stanley Gardner, Rex Stout, and many others—gave readers what they wanted. The period was known as "The Classical Age" of mystery fiction.

Then Dashiell Hammett and Raymond Chandler created their sleuths, Sam Spade and Philip Marlowe. These two American writers introduced mystery readers to the "mean streets" and the flesh-and-blood people who inhabited them. They created the "hardboiled" mystery, in which gritty settings, three-dimensional characters, true-to-life dialogue, irony, mood, style and pace were grafted onto the classical detective puzzle.

In other words, Chandler and Hammett gave us *novels*, mysteries that qualified as genuine works of literature, not merely clever puzzles.

Today's mystery shelves are packed with a rich variety of novels. Contemporary mysteries come in all sizes, styles, themes, and moods—the classic private-eye puzzles of Sue Grafton and Robert B. Parker, the dark brooding novels of James Lee Burke and Lawrence Block, the medical mysteries of Patricia D. Cornwell and Michael Palmer, the police procedurals of Ed McBain and William J. Caunitz, the small-town domestic tales of Katherine Hall Page and Charlotte MacLeod.

But regardless of their genres and sub-genres, contemporary mysteries all contain the same elements:

1. *The puzzle.* The important question that drives the plot of every mystery novel and short story is: Who did it? Who committed the crime (generally murder)? At the beginning, neither the reader nor the story's protagonist knows the answer.

2. *Detection.* The investigation of the crime constitutes the story's central action. When the puzzle is solved, the story ends.

3. *The sleuth as hero.* The protagonist is the character who solves the puzzle, generally through his intelligence, perseverance, courage, physical strength, moral conviction, or a combination of these qualities.

4. *The worthy villain.* The antagonist, generally the murderer, tests the limits of the sleuth's abilities. The villain is clever, resourceful, and single-mindedly intent on getting away with his crime. He makes the puzzle a supreme challenge for both the sleuth and the reader.

5. *Fair play.* All of the evidence uncovered by the sleuth, in the form of clues, is equally available to the reader. The climactic revelation presents no evidence that hasn't already been disclosed in the course of the story.

6. *Realism and logic.* Everything fits, makes sense, and *could* happen the way it's depicted in the story. Mystery stories take place in actual places, or fictional places that seem real. They are populated with characters who resemble real people. Readers care about these characters, engage them emotionally, and feel as if they know them.

In the fifty years since Hammett and Chandler, thousands of literary murders have been solved by hundreds of sleuths in every corner of the globe. There are so many different styles and approaches to the contemporary mystery that terms such as "police procedural," "private eye," "hard-boiled," "soft-boiled," and "cozy," just to name the most obvious, have evolved to help classify them. There are series and non-series mysteries. They take place in the present, in historical eras, even in the future. They are wry and witty, dark and violent, philosophical and urbane.

Fictional detectives range from professionals (police officers, private investigators, lawyers, district attorneys, forensic pathologists, newspaper reporters—those who get paid specifically to investigate murders) to schoolteachers, housewives, teenagers, and other amateurs. They can be female or male, gay or straight, old or young, rich or poor. They work in big cities, suburbs, rural areas, and the wilderness in every state and virtually every nation in the world.

Mystery novels by Tony Hillerman, Sue Grafton, Dick Francis, Barbara Michaels, Robert Parker, Patricia Cornwell, and many others regularly appear on the bestseller lists. Hundreds of other talented writers produce a popular mystery novel every year or two. Many critics contend that some of the very best novel and short-story writers in America and England these days are those who produce mystery fiction.

Every year dozens of "first mysteries" are published. Periodicals such as *Ellery Queen's Mystery Magazine* and *Alfred Hitchcock Mystery Magazine* are devoted exclusively to short mystery fiction. Editors and publishers continually search for the next popular writer, the next blockbuster mystery novel.

The basic elements of mystery fiction remain constant.

Mystery variants

If the story's driving question is not "who did it?," and if detection is not the central action of the story, it is not, technically, a mystery. Today's best-seller lists are often top-heavy with high-suspense titles in which the plot's momentum comes from different questions, typically: "Will the bad guy succeed in carrying out his sinister plan before the good guy can stop him?" John Grisham, Mary Higgins Clark, and Tom Clancy, among many others, have made these "thrillers" enormously popular. Crime and justice are central issues in these novels. Since clues, detection, and puzzle-solving frequently play important, if secondary, parts of their plots, many of the principles of mystery fiction apply equally to them.

The reader as participant

Contemporary mystery fiction invites readers to join the sleuth in the quest to solve a compelling puzzle. Modern readers will not settle for the role of spectator. They want to participate in your story.

Give your readers credit. Assume they are as smart as you are. "No one can write decently," said E. B. White, "who is distrustful of the reader's intelligence, or whose attitude is patronizing."

The most important advice I can give you is this: *Always think of your audience. Write for your readers. Never deprive them of the chance to participate.*

As we have seen, modern readers expect fair play. You cannot withhold vital clues from them. Everything of consequence that your sleuth encounters must also be encountered by your readers. Unless readers have the evidence, they cannot fairly participate in the solving of the puzzle.

On the other hand, readers don't want to be guided through the puzzle's solution. They want only a fair chance to solve it *for themselves*. They don't want to be given more information than the sleuth has. That would give them an advantage over him, which also violates the rule of fair play. Readers resent having clues explained to them by an all-knowing author as much as they resent having clues withheld from them.

Invite them to walk beside your hero or heroine, seeing, hearing, smelling, tasting and feeling along with your sleuth. No more, no less.

Showing without telling

For mystery writers, the golden rule is: *Show, don't tell*. Give your readers the same kinds of sensory impressions they use in their own lives to interpret their world. Then let them draw their own conclusions. When you explain or elaborate for your readers, you deprive them of the opportunity to participate.

Let your readers encounter your story's characters and situations as they experience their actual lives. When you meet and interact with other people, you *observe* their behavior and then you *interpret* it. People's actions and words are clues to their inner feelings, attitudes, philosophies, and motives. You draw conclusions about others based on the clues they present to you. If you see a man crying, you might conclude that he is sad, or frustrated, or angry, or even happy. You take into account the context of his behavior and everything else you know about him—including the possibility that he might lie to you. Then you make your interpretation. You have no all-knowing narrator to tell you, "He is crying tears of joy" or "He is depressed because he killed his friend."

If a woman slams her fist on a tabletop or curses loudly or clenches her teeth, you might conclude that she's angry. You might be wrong. In fact, she might be trying to make you *believe* she's angry when, in fact, she is trying to manipulate your emotions or make you believe something that isn't true. You can't be sure. You have to consider the clues—the observed behavior and everything else you know about that person—to arrive at your best interpretation. In actual life, no narrator stands at your shoulder whispering in your ear, "That person is angry" or "She's only pretending to be angry."

Just as you *show* your readers the characters in your stories, so should you create settings for them. *Show* your readers a restaurant with a jukebox playing a Patti Page tune, candles in Chianti bottles, and red-and-white-checked oilcloth tablecloths, then allow them to draw their own conclusions about the place. Do not *tell* them, "The restaurant had an old-fashioned '50s atmosphere." Readers can—and want to—deduce that for themselves.

Words such as "sad," "manipulative," and "old-fashioned" tell readers more than they want to know. Let them draw their own conclusions, the way they do in real life. Otherwise you'll turn your readers into passive spectators—and turn them off.

Make your story a series of experiences for your readers. Give them sensory impressions. *Show* them some significant details of people and places, but resist the impulse to tell them what those details mean. Write scenes in which characters act and interact, and put your readers in the middle of those scenes. Allow them to participate, to interpret, to draw conclusions, and to fill in the blanks. Trust them to think for themselves. Respect their intelligence.

Showing without telling gives contemporary readers what they want from a mystery story—a fair chance to participate in the puzzle's solution.

≈ 2 ≈

Finding Your Story

THE QUESTION WRITERS are most often asked by non-writers is: "Where do you get your ideas?"

Typically, writers reply, "Why, ideas are everywhere. The newspapers. Television. Cocktail party conversation. Dreams. The problem isn't finding ideas. The problem is recognizing those that can be converted into a story, and then knowing how to create that story."

Sometimes they just smile and say, "Serendipity."

The most honest answer to the question is: "Ideas come from inside my head. If you want a story idea, that's where you have to look."

Sure, there are plenty of ideas. But the workable idea, the one that will sustain a compelling mystery plot, is rare and precious. To recognize a good idea and develop it into a story requires a lot of hard, critical thought and planning.

Sometimes writers are fired by the inspiration of what strikes them as a good idea and are so eager to begin writing that they don't stop to think. They rush to their keyboards and begin writing. They expect their idea to sustain them. They are devastated when, after a few pages or a few chapters, they run out of steam. Their idea did not sustain them, because they failed to nurture and develop it into a fully imagined story.

Planning your story requires more than the inspiration of a good idea. The creative process that precedes actual writing is unique to each writer. Here's how I do it:

Brady Coyne, the lawyer-sleuth hero of my mystery series, likes to ponder difficult cases from the banks of a trout stream or the little balcony off his waterfront apartment in Boston. The process is identical to what I, his creator, go through trying to think up puzzles for him to solve:

I drank and smoked and thought. The breeze came at me from the sea, moist and organic. The bell buoy out there clanged its mournful rhythm. From behind me came the muffled city noises—the wheeze of traffic through the nighttime streets, the occasional punctuation of siren and horn, the almost subsonic hum and murmur of dense human life.

I remembered the Vermont woods, and my picnic with Kat, and how the birds and bugs and animals and river sounded, and how the pine forest smelled, and how my rainbow trout never missed his mayfly.

And while one part of my mind registered all of these surface things and wandered freely on its own associations, a different part of it looked for pattern and purpose in three North Shore murders, and a third part watched what was going on and tried not to judge it or guide it.

That, as well as I can state it, is how I think through a story idea. It's a process of disciplined free association, at once random and purposeful. If anyone watched me do it, they'd accuse me of daydreaming.

I do it on long automobile trips. I tend to miss highway exits when I'm driving. During conversations, I find myself saying, "Excuse me. What were you saying?" Sometimes I lie on my bed and stare at the insides of my eyelids. Now and then I scribble a note about a character or a place or an event on a scrap of paper. Periodically I enter my notes into my computer. I build scenes around them and explore them and try to see where they lead.

More often than not they take me to a dead end. I expect that and keep at it. A good idea is worth working for.

An idea isn't a plot, and a plot isn't a story. An idea is a spark that ignites the individual creative imagination. It can usually be stated in a simple declarative statement, such as, "An elderly woman dying of cancer yearns to reconcile with her estranged daughter before she dies."

Or, "The owner of a million-dollar stamp, thought to be the only one of its kind in existence, is contacted by someone who claims to possess a duplicate of that stamp."

You may not find either of these ideas particularly promising. But I did, and I developed each of them into a novel. An idea that excites me may not strike your imagination, for the obvious reason that you and I have different interests and experiences.

An idea sets off a complicated chain reaction, a sequence of imagined events which the writer converts into scenes populated by imaginary people. That is a plot. When the writer puts it all onto paper, it becomes a story.

In their search for ideas, some mystery writers hang around with newspaper reporters, or sit in courtrooms, or lurk in barrooms, or ride with police officers. I know one writer who tunes in the afternoon television talk shows. He claims he's gotten several story ideas from the oddball people interviewed by Oprah and Donahue.

Always be alert for ideas. Read compulsively and eclectically. Eavesdrop shamelessly. Visit new places. Study people. Engage strangers in conversation. And when you get an idea that excites you, resist the powerful temptation to sit down immediately and start writing. Instead, find a quiet place where you can practice the discipline of controlled free association.

The best way to create a complex mystery plot from a single exciting idea is to keep asking yourself: "What if?" Here's an example of how this works for me:

The idea for my first novel, *Death at Charity's Point*, came from the news story of a fugitive from the law who, after several years of living quietly under an assumed identity, a pillar of his little rural community, decided to turn himself in.

What if, I asked myself, someone in this fugitive's little community had uncovered his true identity? And *what if* he didn't want to be brought to justice? *What if* he committed murder to protect his secret?

This struck me as a promising idea for a mystery novel. I stated it for myself in the form of a premise: "A former '60s radical, wanted by the FBI and living under an assumed identity, commits murder to protect her secret." I then bombarded the premise with more what-if questions. *What if* the murder appeared to be a suicide? *What if* the victim's elderly mother refused to believe her son would take his own life? *What if* she engaged the family lawyer to investigate? *What if* the murderer committed more murders? *What if* she targeted the lawyer for death?

Asking those "what if" questions often felt random and unproductive. For every useful answer, dozens led nowhere. But I kept asking them until I believed I had a coherent story. Then I created and revised outlines, wrote character sketches, and explored possible settings.

The source of my idea had been televised nationally. But as far as I know, no one else used it as the basis for a mystery novel. It worked for me because it merged with that unique entity that is my imagination, which is the product of my peculiar history, personality, and life experiences.

And if it had happened to inspire someone else, their novel would without doubt have been unrecognizably different from mine.

The formula that generally works for me is: CHARACTER + PROBLEM = STORY IDEA. The character is usually either a murderer or the victim of a murderer. That character's story becomes the basis for the novel. But it's not the novel itself.

The two stories of the mystery

Mystery fiction, remember, tells a tale of detection. It's a puzzle. It raises the "whodunit" question and sets the sleuth off on her quest. Along the way she encounters clues until she—and the reader—have learned enough to solve the puzzle.

Before you write this story of detection, *you must first write the story of the murder itself.* It's a chronological tale. It begins with the relationship between the victim and the murderer, explains the murderer's motive, and develops through the planning and execution of the deed.

What clues will you scatter along the way? What other innocent characters are associated with the victim? Might they, too, have motive, means, and opportunity to commit murder? How has the culprit covered his tracks? What are the relationships among all of these characters? Where does the story take place? How do elements in the setting contribute to the story's events?

Answering all of these questions will give you a story of murder.

Write a narrative sketch of this straightforward tale.

Tell it chronologically. Populate it with husbands and wives, lovers and ex-spouses, business acquaintances and estranged friends. Compose the life story of your victim. Be sure he has plenty of potential enemies. Then do the same for your murderer.

This sketch could itself be the plot for a novel. With fascinating multi-dimensional characters, complex relationships, a powerful underlying moral question, a touch of irony, and intense conflicts, it might even make a very good suspense novel or thriller.

But because this is the story of the villain and his victim, it's not yet a mystery. The mystery story belongs to the sleuth.

To create a mystery, you must convert the linear murderer-victim story into a puzzle and create a puzzle-solving hero. This is the specific challenge for the mystery writer. You must invent two stories for every one you write. First you must think up the story of the crime. Only then can you write your mystery novel, *which is the story of that crime's detection.*

Book-length mysteries are, in all respects, *novels.* A mystery novel, just like a "literary novel," should be populated with fascinating multi-dimensional characters. It should ask important moral questions. Mystery fiction, every bit as much as the mainstream variety, can explore the complexity of the human spirit and the irony of the human condition. The best ones do exactly that.

But mystery fiction offers a bonus. The bonus is the puzzle.

Here's how I constructed the two stories that became my eleventh Brady Coyne novel, *Tight Lines:*

I decided to explore the difficult and intense relationships that inevitably develop between psychiatrists and their patients in the course of psychoanalysis. Patients, in some cases, fall in love with and may attempt to seduce their analysts, whose professional ethic requires them to resist powerful temptations while continuing to treat their patients. This doctor-patient relationship was the idea for my story.

Sometimes psychiatrists succumb to temptation. "What if," I thought, "a psychiatrist had an affair with his beautiful female patient?"

And, because my story had to be a mystery, I next asked: "What if that patient were murdered?"

The storyline that resulted went this way: Mary Ellen Ames worshipped her father, who died when she was in college. Mary Ellen cut off ties with her mother and proceeded to engage in a series of love affairs with older men, many of them married. She became involved with drugs and had a homosexual encounter. After several years she decided to seek psychiatric help. She chose Dr. Warren McAllister, a middle-aged psychoanalyst who reminded her of her father, gradually seduced him, and then threatened to expose him to his wife and his professional associates if he didn't agree to marry her.

I thought hard and long about Mary Ellen Ames and Warren McAllister and his wife. I created Mary Ellen's lovers—the married college professor, the bookstore owner who supplied her with drugs, the suspended Boston policeman who lived in a trailer, the troubled young woman who lived in Mary Ellen's apartment building. I gave Mary Ellen's mother a story, too. She lived alone in the Ames family mansion. She was suffering from terminal cancer and wanted to reconcile with her estranged daughter before she died.

From this lineup of characters I selected a murderer.

Then I was ready to write a detailed narrative summary of this story, complete with all of the characters' life histories, personalities, and strongly felt needs and desires. The process took me several weeks of difficult and frustrating trial-and-error thinking.

Only when I felt I knew this story thoroughly did I begin converting it into a mystery novel which, I knew, would be propelled by the puzzle question: Who killed Mary Ellen Ames?

Because I have a series character, my lawyer Brady Coyne had to serve as the puzzle-solver. So the first question I had to answer was: How would Brady get involved with the case?

I decided that Susan Ames would ask Brady, her family lawyer, to track down her daughter. The story of detection was underway.

Then came the puzzle's development, the unfolding of clues, false trails, and red herrings. Brady tries to track down Mary Ellen. He learns where she lives, but she hasn't been home in more than a week. He convinces the building's superintendent to let him into Mary Ellen's apartment, where he finds a bottle of prescription medicine. This leads him to Dr. McAllister, the psychiatrist, who eventually confides in Brady that he's been having an affair with Mary Ellen but insists that he doesn't know where she is.

Eventually, Mary Ellen's body is found in a New Hampshire pond. Based on the medical examiner's report, the police call it an accidental drowning, but Brady has his doubts. By now, he's encountered some of the people in Mary Ellen's life, all of whom could have a motive for murdering the young woman.

As Brady investigates, the stakes grow higher. What began as a search for a missing woman becomes a desperate race against time and a murderer who will kill again. Ultimately, Brady finds himself endangered.

And so forth, to the ultimate revelation.

I wrote a narrative summary of this story of detection, too, taking elements of the first storyline and placing them into the second. I laid out the story's various turning points—the opening scene with the dying mother, Brady's encounters with each of the people in Mary Ellen's life, the discovery of Mary Ellen's body. I converted facts from the first story into clues, dead-end trails, false suspects, and misleading assumptions.

As the story took shape, it transformed itself into a sequence of scenes, each of which moved the story forward, introduced new information, raised new questions, complicated the puzzle, and jacked up the stakes.

When I summarized all of the scenes, I was ready to write the book. I knew my story. I had direction and purpose.

Of course, some things changed. As the characters began to participate in actual scenes, they came to life. I discovered that some of them had depths and contradictions and motivations I hadn't originally imagined, which suggested modifications in the plot. I was receptive to changes, but skeptical, too; I considered them carefully before incorporating them into my story.

In the end, when the solution to the puzzle was revealed, I hoped that readers could say that everything fit together, the clues were fair, and they knew as much as Brady did. They had experienced my story as a participant, not a mere spectator. I also hoped they would then say, "I should have figured it out for myself. But it fooled me."

The case of the short story

The elements of mystery short stories are no different from those of novels. No matter how short, every story has a plot, a setting, and characters. It contains a combination of narrative and dialogue. It has a beginning, a middle, and an end.

To say that a short story is the same as the novel except that it is shorter, however, is to ignore some fundamental differences between the two forms. The short story makes special demands on the writer.

Some of these demands are relatively obvious. The short story involves just a few characters—perhaps only one or two. It typically uses only one setting and a single point of view. It occurs over a short period of time— often as a single event that unfolds without interruption. Descriptions are spare. Characters and settings are drawn with a few deft strokes. Every detail must serve a purpose. Dialogue is spare and to the point.

In other words, nothing is wasted in the short story, which typically runs from 1,500 to 5,000 words—twenty or more times shorter than an average novel. Regardless of the story's length, the writer must strive to make every paragraph, every sentence, every word serve a purpose. Rarely can the short story accommodate extended descriptive passages or flashbacks, rambling dialogue, extraneous secondary characters, or subplots. Short stories can be difficult and time-consuming to write, but they are meant to be read in a single uninterrupted sitting. The short story contains a single, focused narrative purpose.

The "purpose" of the short story is to dramatize just one point, which can usually be stated as the story's theme: Crime doesn't pay (or, crime sometimes *does* pay); a crisis will bring out the best (or the worst) in people; revenge is sweet (or bitter); love conquers all (or hatred conquers love). The story is written with the single-minded aim of dramatizing its point. It teaches a lesson in human nature, it contains a moral, it offers an insight.

The payoff of the mystery short story comes in the form of a surprise or twist at the climax. It gives the reader a "punch." The entire story is written to dramatize the meaning of that climactic revelation.

Anything that does not contribute to maximizing the impact of the punch should be eliminated.

The punch of most mystery short stories dramatizes the simple theme that things are not what they appear to be. In the classical whodunit story, for example, the most likely suspect is innocent (although in the focused, economical short story, the actual villain may not be revealed if that is not the story's point). Other mystery storylines focus on the discovery of an unexpected motive for murder, or the surprising meaning of a single puzzling clue, or the unforeseen relationship between the villain and the victim, or a revealing event in one character's past.

Things are not what they seem. Dramatizing what they actually are is the story's point. It offers the reader a new insight—into human nature, into the ironies of life, into the meaning of love, or hate, or death, or greed. After reading an effective short story, the reader should stop for a moment and think, "Ah, yes. I never thought of it that way before."

The short story contains the same structural elements as the novel:

1. Situation—Virtually all fiction of any length focuses on an interesting character with a problem. A detective is hired to solve a crime. A murderer attempts to escape detection. A husband seeks to find his missing wife. A compulsive gambler seeks to win back everything he's lost. Short-story situations can be less dramatic and highly charged than those that move novels. The situation in a short story is often commonplace, something that the average reader can identify with. But the situ-

ation must be important to the story's protagonist, whose goal (to resolve the problem) gives momentum to the story.

2. Complication—The situation creates the story's motivation. It forces the character to act to achieve his or her goal. This action produces more and greater problems. Obstacles arise in the form of a new situation and/or another character (the antagonist) who opposes the protagonist.

3. Climax—The protagonist arrives at the crisis, the turning point in the action, the moment when he or she must make the right decision or fail to achieve his or her goal.

4. Resolution—If the protagonist took the right actions, the problem is solved. If not, the problem remains unresolved, or even more complicated than it was at the beginning, depending on the point the story is making. In any case, the story's resolution must relate directly to the situation it began with, and it must result directly from the actions of the protagonist.

You can achieve interesting short-story effects by altering the natural chronological order in which these structural elements occur. For example, you can begin with the climax (the moment when the protagonist must decide whether to break into his boss's office or walk away) or even the resolution (the protagonist is being pronounced guilty by the jury), then tell the rest of the story as flashback. Or you can use the complication (the protagonist is confronted by the antagonist) as your narrative hook.

Many mystery writers find the short story form, with all of its constraints and demands, more difficult than the novel. They think in terms of novel-length fiction, and when an idea attracts them, they develop and complicate it for the novel form. Others are drawn to the focus and discipline of the short story. Most writers, however, agree that the short-story form forces them to write well, and for this reason alone, even if your goal is to publish a novel, you should try to write short stories.

≈ 3 ≈

The Protagonist:
The Sleuth As
Hero Or Heroine

A<small>N EDITOR REJECTED</small> my first novel with these words: "I think it would take something really unusual to convince us to take on a new mystery series—an Armenian/Jewish plumber who solves cases by listening at people's drain pipes, or something like that."

The point, of course, was this: Publishers—and readers—look for unusual and fascinating protagonists. In fact, in mystery fiction appealing sleuths are at least as important as clever storylines.

A compelling protagonist can sell an ordinary plot. Characters make stories seem real. Readers invest their emotions in characters, not plots. They experience strong feelings—happiness, sadness, anger, worry, fear—because they care about what happens to the characters.

In the case of mystery fiction, the character readers care most about is the sleuth.

A mystery plot is basically the story of the hero or heroine's problems. The most compelling problem, of course, is the puzzle, the "whodunit" question. Mystery storylines are driven by the process of detection. The story belongs to the detective. The sleuth is the one with the problem.

In the mystery, things happen because the protagonist *makes* them happen. Your heroine is the story's catalyst. She is active, not reactive. She doesn't sit around waiting for things to happen to her. She works hard to uncover and interpret clues—they are never given to her gratuitously. She is not passive. She desperately wants to solve the puzzle, and she strives passionately to do it. She has goals and she struggles against powerful obstacles to achieve them. She takes risks, confronts threats, and doesn't quit.

Things are never easy for the heroine or hero.

Make your readers worry about your protagonist and you've got them all the way to The End.

The mystery is a quest story. The sleuth strives to uncover a villain who doesn't want to be uncovered and will do anything—even murder the sleuth—to prevent it. The mystery builds tension and suspense as the sleuth confronts danger in pursuit of the quest.

The sleuth typically has many of the characteristics of the mythical hero—purity of purpose, courage, conviction, and single-minded commitment to ideals. John D. MacDonald's Travis McGee, for example, thinks of himself as a crusader. In *The Dreadful Lemon Sky*, MacDonald writes:

It is unseemly to feel festive about checking out the death of a dead friend. But there is something heartening about having a sense of mission. A clean purpose. A noble intent, no matter how foolish. . . . Ahead, some murky mystery locked in the broken skull of a dead lady. The knight errant, earning his own self-esteem, holding the palms cupped to make a dragon trap.

The stories of most successful mystery writers similarly hinge on their hero or heroine setting off to solve a mystery with a "sense of mission," a "clean purpose," and a "noble intent." Robert Parker's Spenser is clearly a hero from the Travis McGee mold. So, in their own ways, are Sue Grafton's Kinsey Millhone, Sara Paretsky's V. I. Warshawski, Lawrence Block's Matt Scudder, and many others.

Think of your sleuth as a noble—but human and accessible—knight errant. Make your mystery stories journeys—for your hero or heroine, for your readers, and for yourself.

This is the storyline of virtually every successful mystery story: The sleuth has big problems, and as the story unfolds, these problems grow bigger and more baffling and dangerous. But the sleuth perseveres.

Readers convert the sleuth's quest into a question: Will he or she succeed? Make readers care, keep them in doubt, and you'll keep them reading.

Mystery heroes and heroines can be many things— lawyers, hairdressers, children, or Armenian plumbers—but they cannot be weak-willed, passive, or indecisive. Sleuths make things happen. They do not wait for things to happen to them. They succeed because they're aggressive and stubborn—not because they're lucky.

Mystery protagonists, in other words, are not wimps.

Auguste Dupin and Sherlock Holmes weren't wimps, nor were Nero Wolfe or Sam Spade, Philip Marlowe or Travis McGee, Perry Mason or Mike Hammer. Sue Grafton's Kinsey Millhone and Sara Paretsky's V. I. Warshawski aren't wimps. Neither are Tony Hillerman's

Jim Chee or Patricia Cornwell's Kay Scarpetta or any of Ed McBain's cops at the 87th Precinct.

Idiosyncratic, yes. Distinctive, definitely. Flawed, human, and accessible. Some heroes and heroines welcome physical confrontations, while others prefer mental contests. But none of them is a wimp.

Study these and other protagonists of successful mystery fiction. I guarantee you'll find them all strong-willed, capable, smart, admirable, persevering, and likeable—the kind of people that readers respect, identify with, and root for. Mystery sleuths know what they're after, they want it badly, and they take risks to achieve it.

This does not mean that heroes and heroines must be bigger than life. If they never fail, or if they're know-it-alls, the outcome of their quest will never be in doubt, and your story will lack tension and suspense. They can—and should—have blind spots, quirks, and weaknesses which they must struggle to overcome. Their human limitations make them appealing to readers and complicate their quest.

The sleuth you create is as important to the success of your story as the plot.

First you must give him or her a job.

The professional sleuth

The professionals who get paid specifically to solve murders include homicide cops, private investigators, criminal lawyers, prosecuting attorneys, newspaper or television reporters, and forensic pathologists. Their motivation is never in doubt. They investigate murders because that's how they earn a living, and they do it relentlessly and well because they are committed and talented.

The professional sleuth is an otherwise ordinary person whose job happens to involve investigating murders. He may be an overweight recovering alcoholic with an ex-wife who haunts him for alimony and estranged children he never sees and colleagues who refuse to cooperate with him. She may live in a run-down trailer park, be pestered by an amorous vacuum-cleaner salesman, suffer from menopause, smoke mentholated cigarettes, own an ancient Volkswagen with bad brakes, and live on Diet Coke and Tums.

Professional sleuths persevere regardless of their problems. If they didn't, they wouldn't be effective fictional heroines and heroes.

For one thing, they need the money. That's a good start, but it's not enough. Other powerful motivations such as loyalty, anger, love, or fear drive them.

The higher the stakes for your sleuth—the more he or she stands to gain or lose—the more compelling your story will be, and the faster your reader will turn the pages.

The writer whose sleuth is a professional has a built-in solution to the problem of how to get the story's quest underway. Chapter One opens when an elderly man walks into the office, slumps into a chair, and says: "My wife is missing. I'll pay you to find her. I'll pay you whatever you want."

Or the chief of detectives growls: "Senator Smith's body was found floating in the river last night. He was shot three times in the face. Find out who murdered him, and do it fast. Your promotion depends on it."

Or the editor says: "A bomb exploded in a convenience store. Three people died. Get the story and get it today, or I'll find someone else who will."

Thus do professionals begin their investigation. Their reputations, their self-esteem, their careers, and perhaps their lives are at stake.

Your story has begun.

If you decide your hero or heroine will be a professional, you must be thoroughly familiar with that profession. Don't try to fake it. Every detail must be absolutely accurate. Your cop must think like a cop, talk like a cop, and behave like a cop. Your lawyer must know the law. Your reporter must know how to meet a deadline. Your pathologist must know medicine.

When you write a mystery story, you and your reader make a bargain: Your reader agrees to pretend that your story actually happened, provided you agree to make your story resemble reality. A single misstep or false note will break the contract by shattering your readers' faith—their "willing suspension of disbelief."

The amateur sleuth

An amateur sleuth—a person whose livelihood does not depend on investigating murders—can, at least in theory, come from any walk of life. Housewives and kindergarten teachers, secretaries and bartenders, jockeys and tennis players, computer nerds and real estate brokers—all can find themselves in situations where they might need to solve a murder. A husband might be driven to find his wife's killer, for example, and readers will readily believe that a parent would stop at nothing to track down the kidnapper of a child.

The challenge for the writer is to give amateur sleuths powerfully compelling reasons to pursue their own investigations instead of hiring a professional.

They must be strongly driven to persevere, even when the stakes get higher and the risks multiply. If readers don't buy the amateur sleuth's motive, the story, no matter how clever and dramatic it might otherwise be, will flop.

The motive should result from the story's events, not

your sleuth's personality. It's not enough to portray your hero or heroine as naturally curious or brave or persistent. You must create a situation that compels even the most reluctant protagonist to take action.

Since amateurs bring no necessary experience or expertise to the murder investigation, the writer who decides on an amateur can usually avoid the intense research that goes into creating a believable professional.

If you give your amateur hero a convincing reason to chase down a murderer no matter what the danger, a reason that readers can empathize with, you'll sink your hook in deep.

The amateur is likely to change more than the professional as she pursues her investigation. The amateur has probably never before been particularly courageous or resourceful or persevering, and certainly has never had to track down a killer. Now she is forced into a situation that tests her will and courage and intelligence as they have never been tested before.

Gender, appearance, and other characteristics

Your sleuth can be old or young, rich or poor, gay or straight, lighthearted or gloomy, strong or weak, attractive or plain. There are no formulas and no taboos.

James Lee Burke's Dave Robicheaux is a recovering alcoholic. Barbara Neely's Blanche White is an African-American housekeeper. Lawrence Block's Bernie Rhodenbarr is a burglar who runs a bookstore. Jake Page's Mo Bowdre is a blind sculptor. Dana Stabenow's Kate Shugak is an Alaskan Aleut detective. Tony Hillerman's Jim Chee and Joe Leaphorn are Navajo policemen. Linda Barnes' Carlotta Carlyle plays volleyball and drives a cab. Robert Parker's Spenser is a weight-lifter and a gourmet cook. Katherine Hall Page's Faith Fairchild is the wife of a minister and a former New York caterer. All are popular and memorable sleuths.

Mix and match gender, job, hobby, personal history, appearance, and other characteristics to create your own unique, complex, multi-dimensional sleuth.

The series sleuth

The recurring hero or heroine is a staple of mystery fiction. When considering a first novel for publication, acquiring editors often base their decision on the promise of future novels with the same sleuth. They know that readers develop strong loyalties to appealing heroines and heroes. Mystery readers often care as much about the sleuth's personal problems as they do about the puzzle she's working on.

But the series sleuth must be designed for the long haul. If your first novel features a librarian as a protagonist, you'd better be able to convince an editor that your librarian is an internationally renowned expert in rare and valuable books who is periodically called upon to consult in cases of theft and forgery.

A psychologist whose specialty is child abuse, such as Jonathan Kellerman's Alexander Delaware, makes an effective series hero. So does Rick Boyer's Doc Adams, a forensic dentist. An auto mechanic who's an expert at identifying stolen vehicles could be a series hero. So could a professor of sociology who wrote her doctoral dissertation on rape, or a museum curator or an antique collector whose expertise makes them useful advisers to those who investigate crimes for a living. But unless you give your series sleuth an area of specialization that could logically involve her in mystery puzzles, you will be hard-pressed to think up an entire series of cases for her.

If you intend to write a series, then make your sleuth

either a professional (private investigator, police officer, crime reporter, lawyer) or an amateur with special crime-busting credentials.

But you have to sell your first book before you need to begin worrying about a series. If you've dreamed up a can't-miss storyline that demands an amateur one-shot hero, that's the book you should write. Elmore Leonard and Dick Francis and many other successful mystery authors create new heroes for every story. They thereby avoid the trap that ensnared Conan Doyle, who became so bored with Sherlock Holmes that he killed him off. Eventually Doyle was forced to revive his famous detective when readers made it clear that they wanted only Holmes stories from him.

Defining characters by what they want

Your sleuth should obviously be drawn with the greatest care. You want your readers to identify with her, root for her, agonize with her when she fails, exult with her when she triumphs. Make them care about her happiness and her health and her success. Make them wonder how she's getting along with her ex-husband or lover. Make them hope she'll have a chance to take a vacation, or play more tennis, or visit her father in the nursing home. You want readers to wish your sleuth would eat more sensibly and quit smoking and finally settle down with that elusive young policeman.

Making readers bring these concerns to your books doesn't happen by accident. In the process of developing mystery heroes and heroines, you must explore their full range of interests, desires, needs, and fears.

Everything that goes into characterizing your sleuth can be expressed in terms of *what she wants*. Readers will worry about her because she has goals that are important to her and it's not certain that she'll achieve them.

Every mystery hero or heroine, like every real person, has several needs and desires. These goals may conflict with each other and with those of other characters. Such conflicts lend depth and texture to your story. Your sleuth, for example, may *want* to follow the trail of a killer from Chicago to Baltimore. But he also *wants* his wife to be happy, and she doesn't *want* him to leave her home alone to watch over their wayward teen-aged son (who *wants* to skip school and experiment with marijuana).

But your readers would not be satisfied with a novel about your sleuth unless a whodunit puzzle is its focus. In every novel, no matter what other problems your heroine has to confront, she *wants* above all to solve a crime.

This purpose supersedes all of her other goals. If it didn't, she'd go visit her father or play tennis instead of tracking down the bad guy.

Define your story by your sleuth's motivation. What does she want? Why does she want it so badly? Why does she care enough to take significant risks to attain it?

Then identify your villain's goals, and make sure that his wants are strongly felt and in direct conflict with your sleuth's.

Mystery novels focus on the needs and goals of their characters: The sleuth wants to unravel the clues, identify the villain, and bring him to justice; the villain wants to elude the hero, escape detection, and get away with murder. Many of your characters' goals will not be readily apparent to your readers. Those that are hidden help to create the story's mystery. Deducing the true aims of the villain, for example, typically forms a vital part of the story of detection.

For each important goal, decide *why* the character needs or wants it so much. Then create scenes that suggest those goals. Your characters' actions are clues to their goals.

A mystery plot can be understood as an evenly matched game between protagonist and antagonist. The stakes are high. Both have important goals and want desperately to achieve them. But it's a zero-sum game. If the hero or heroine wins, the villain must lose.

Creating character profiles

Write down everything you can think of about your characters. Your hero or heroine, your villain, and your other central characters deserve fully developed biographies. Include family histories, birthplaces, schooling, marriages, personal triumphs and tragedies. Think of what your characters like to read and eat and the music they enjoy. What are their politics and their opinions on current issues? How do they like to spend their leisure time? What do they worry about? What do they believe in?

Visualize them. How old are they? What do they look like? What kinds of clothes do they wear?

Imagine their surroundings, too. Draw a word sketch of their house or apartment and their office. Is it neat or cluttered? What paintings hang on the walls? What magazines are on the coffee table?

All of this creative work is background, the writer's necessary homework. You must know your characters fully before you write about them. But be prepared to leave much of this biographical material out of your story.

After creating a dramatic opening scene in which a corpse is discovered and your sleuth appears, you might be tempted to interrupt your story to tell your readers all about your hero:

> He peered into the mirror, scraping his razor carefully around the raised red scar that ran from the corner of his mouth to his jaw, and he remembered that fateful night in New Orleans when Millie O'Leary, the blonde in the black velvet dress, with the glass eye. . .

And if you're not careful, you'll allow your character to remember all of the delightful material from that biography you worked so hard to create. From the night in New Orleans, you'll recount your hero's childhood, and how the playground bully always stole his lunch money, and how his father said that if he ever wanted to be a man he'd have to learn to stand up to bullies and defend himself. His mother hated violence, and Mom and Dad had big arguments about it. Your hero knew that it was his fault that his parents fought all the time, so he secretly joined a gym and met an ex-prizefighter, who . . .

And so on and on and on. By now your readers have completely lost track of your story and are likely to set your book aside.

Don't allow the biographies you've composed to limit your imagination and creativity. If, once your story is under way, you find that your characters begin saying and doing unexpected things, don't resist them. Characters often do "come alive" in the story as they never do in sketches and biographies.

Characterization through scenes

In real life, the more we listen to people talk and watch them act, the more we know about them. The same is true in fiction.

Mystery readers prefer to learn about fictional characters the way they get to know real people: by watching them and listening to them.

Everything characters say or do is a clue to their personalities, their life histories, and the forces that motivate them. As they act and speak in scenes, your characters will gradually acquire depth and complexity. Good writers reveal what their characters are like by *showing* them in action.

In a mystery story, of course, things are never what they appear to be. For example, suppose your readers first meet a character named Harry when he enters a tavern. He straddles a stool, nods to the bartender, and says, "Gimme a Bud."

A moment later Mr. Rowan appears. He slides onto the adjacent barstool, adjusts the crease in his pants, and says, "Excuse me, bartender, but what do you have by way of German beers?"

In this simple scene readers will find clues to the education, experience, taste, appearance, and attitudes of two characters. Readers will expect conflict between these two, and as the scene develops they will learn more about them.

As you show Harry and Mr. Rowan interacting with other characters in this and in later scenes, readers may gradually deduce that the crude Harry, in fact, is a philosophy professor, while the well-dressed and cosmopolitan Mr. Rowan is a Mafia hit man. That process of discovery and surprise is what makes mystery stories compelling for readers.

≈ 4 ≈

The Lineup: Villains, Victims, Suspects, and Other Characters

IN MYSTERY FICTION, although several characters might have valid motives for committing a murder, only the villain did it. He kills for compelling—but rarely obvious—reasons, and then uses his considerable intelligence to avoid being detected. He presents a supreme challenge to the detective. He makes no mistakes. He never panics. He leaves no blatant clues behind. He never acts guilty. He lies convincingly. He misdirects anyone who might begin to suspect him. He'll do anything—including committing more murders—to avoid being nabbed.

It's even money he'll get away with it. It will take a clever, resourceful, and determined sleuth—and reader—to identify him and bring him to justice. When you write mystery fiction, if you make it easy, you make it boring.

Readers should meet the villain early in the story. At this point, of course, only the writer knows who the villain is and what he or she has done, or is about to do.

For the mystery writer, the rule is this: Make the villain one of the crowd, neither more nor less prominent than any of the story's other characters.

Only with the climactic revelation do you transform the villain from an ordinary character into one of great complexity. After all, who'd have suspected that she was capable of all those murders?

Beginning writers tend to worry that unless their villain acts guilty, or appears evil, or has a transparent motive, or is obviously stronger or craftier or more unscrupulous than the other characters, they are not playing fair with their readers. Resist the temptation to throw in clues for your readers' benefit while withholding them from your heroine or hero. And never allow your sleuth to miss a clue that is obvious to your reader. That's giving the reader an unfair advantage—and mystery readers don't want an advantage over the sleuth.

If your readers lose respect for your sleuth, you'll lose your readers.

A worthy villain challenges your hero or heroine and leaves the story's outcome in doubt. Match a determined sleuth against a resourceful and clever and equally determined villain and you'll have your readers hooked.

Suspects and red herrings

In the course of pursuing her investigation, your sleuth encounters a variety of characters who are linked to the victim and could have had the means, motive, and opportunity to commit the murder. The more legitimate suspects your story has, and the longer you keep them under suspicion, the more complicated and challenging your puzzle will be.

Don't disappoint your readers by exonerating too many suspects too quickly. Remember: Only one is the actual villain. All the rest are "red herrings," characters who, despite appearances, are innocent and whose main function in the story is to misdirect the reader's attention. But don't introduce red herrings for the sole purpose of misleading your readers. Every character should have a crucial part to play in the story, offering information of some kind that either helps your sleuth gather clues or misdirects her (and your readers). All characters, however minor, must have motives and goals that connect to the victim and the events of the story.

You can test the validity of a suspect by asking this question: If I omitted this character entirely, would my story collapse?

Your answer must be "yes." Otherwise you're not playing fair.

Victims

In some stories, a character's simple function is to trigger the mystery by getting murdered. The sleuth may begin by investigating this murder, but soon more complicated questions arise, and the victim turns out to be a minor character whose significance fades as the story develops.

More often, however, a murder victim has secrets that provide the murderer with a motive. The connection between the victim's secret and the murderer's motive is the solution to the puzzle.

Mystery fiction typically begins with the discovery of a corpse. The victim is already dead, and readers never get to know him directly. Even in stories where the murder occurs after readers have met the victim, they don't know everything about him. An important part of the sleuth's investigation becomes the painstaking piecing together of the victim's backstory, which comes in bits and pieces of information, often seemingly contradictory, filtered through the memories and motives and lies of other characters.

Who *was* this person? What did he do and know? Who'd want to kill him?

You must know the answers to these questions before you begin writing. Next to your hero or heroine, your victims—even if readers first meet them as dead bodies—are often the most important and interesting characters in mystery fiction.

Write the life story of your victim before you begin to write your story of detection. Make it rich and complicated and unusual. Give him or her friends and lovers, opponents and enemies. Above all, give him secrets.

Remember, something absolutely fascinating happened to this character: He got murdered.

Sidekicks, lovers, and friends

Holmes has Watson, Nero Wolfe has Archie, Travis McGee has Meyer, Spenser has Hawk. Every mystery sleuth, like every real-life person, has relatives and lovers, casual acquaintances and best friends, adversaries and enemies. These secondary characters make your sleuth's life full and complex and interesting. Most of them serve several functions at once.

Mystery heroes cannot be in more than one place at a time. They also need sounding boards, trusted friends in whom they can confide, allies who can offer them insights and interpretations, raise doubts, and worry about them. Archie Goodwin, for example, does Nero Wolfe's leg work. Meyer is an economist who can explain complicated business and financial matters to Travis McGee. Hawk opens doors into Boston's criminal nether world for Spenser. Police officers have their snitches and their fellow officers. Reporters have their sources.

The growing and shifting relationships between sleuths and their acquaintances help define them and make them human and accessible to readers. These secondary but important characters offer material for the subplots that deepen and define your sleuth, who may, for example, be a bold and decisive investigator but a hesitant and flawed lover, or who may find himself torn between family commitments and the demands of his investigation.

Relationships and interactions among friends, family members, lovers, business associates, and even rivals will help to define and complicate and individualize your sleuth and add texture to your story. If secondary characters do none of these things, they don't belong there.

Minor characters

Some characters appear once or twice to serve specific story functions. The taxi must have a driver. The gangster has his bodyguard. The politician has a press agent, the business executive a receptionist. When you draw these characters on your pages you can sketch them with a couple of quick strokes, since you know they're unimportant.

But wait. Your readers don't know that these characters aren't, in fact, key players. The Senator's press agent could be the one who hired the hit man to bump off the woman who was blackmailing his boss. The bodyguard might turn out to be an undercover police informant. The receptionist might actually be the CEO's mistress.

Shrewd mystery readers trust no one. Everybody's a suspect. They know that a seemingly minor character can turn out to be the villain.

Don't disappoint them.

You can't—and shouldn't—create elaborate backstories for every taxi driver and waitress who accepts a tip from your hero. Don't exaggerate their importance, and don't introduce them for the sole purpose of complicating your plot and misleading your readers. Play fair. *You* know they're minor.

But recognize every character's potential as a suspect. Make those quick descriptive strokes and snatches of dialogue memorable enough to stick in your reader's mind.

Mystery readers, like writers, enjoy creating and discarding scenarios. Don't deprive them of their fun.

Creating memorable secondary characters

Mystery readers understand that bartenders and secretaries, cousins and stepdaughters, auto mechanics and family doctors—and, in fact, every character who steps onto the page—*could* be a suspect. Readers look for clues to the mystery's solution in these characters. They understand that hastily and carelessly drawn characters, besides being uninteresting, do not make valid suspects. If you ignore the potential of minor characters by making them flat, one-dimensional cut-outs, you will not only write lifeless stories, but you will also deprive yourself—and your readers—of a rich source of suspects.

If all of your characters except the bad guy are caricatures, readers will solve the case too easily. If none of your minor characters is carefully drawn, they will all be instantly eliminated as suspects by discerning readers. In neither case have you fully exploited the opportunity to create the complexity that mystery readers love.

Give even your minor players the depth and texture to be possible suspects. Take care to draw none of them as transparently and one-dimensionally good or bad. Let your readers interpret them with some uncertainty.

The case of the whistling janitor

Your protagonist enters the lobby of an office building, looking for information. He notices a janitor. Who would know the people who work in this building better than a janitor? Who would be in a better position to have seen or overheard things that can help your sleuth?

At this point, your shrewd reader thinks, "Yes, and who would have a better opportunity to commit crimes here?" Your janitor thus becomes an instant suspect if you introduce him cleverly. Only you know for sure whether he's a red herring or the actual villain. Be careful not to give it away too easily. Let your reader wonder about this janitor.

You might proceed this way:

> A janitor wearing a starched gray shirt and matching pants puttered nearby. He looked about seventy. He was short and wiry, with iron-colored hair slicked back tight against his scalp and white stubble sprouting on his cheeks. He chewed an unlit cigar butt with his stumpy gray teeth. He had sad brown eyes and shaggy eyebrows and a long nose that looked as if it had been broken a few times.

Inexperienced writers tend to confuse detailed physical description with deep characterization. In this passage, the writer draws a clear picture of the janitor's physical appearance. But it is a flat, one-dimensional, rather typical portrait that opens no window into the man's character or life.

He's a cliché who offers no surprises, no different from the bubble-headed blonde, the whore with the heart of gold, the wine-guzzling panhandler, or the unscrupulous used-car salesman. Readers yawn at clichéd characters. They've met them before.

Some writers go to the other extreme, writing exaggerated physical descriptions in their effort to create memorable minor characters. They might introduce our janitor this way:

> A janitor wearing a Hawaiian shirt and plaid Bermuda shorts puttered nearby. He was barely five feet tall and weighed at least 300 pounds. He sported a Fu Manchu mustache, and his scalp had been shaved to the skin except for a strip down the center, which was dyed purple and hung behind him in a long ponytail tied with a pink ribbon.

Grotesquely obese (or emaciated) waitresses, seven-foot (or five-foot) lawyers, and purple-haired (or skull-shaven) teenagers, or characters who are incredibly beautiful (or ugly), smart (or stupid), graceful (or awkward), do not strike the reader as true-to-life. At best, they're utterly boring; at worst, they make the narrator or point-of-view character (and, by extension, the author) seem superficial and mean-spirited, and they will alienate rather than attract the reader.

Complicated and interesting characters can be created with quick and simple strokes by giving readers something they don't expect. For example:

> A janitor wearing a starched gray shirt and matching pants puttered nearby. He was pushing a big canvas basket on wheels. He bent close to me and emptied an ashtray into his basket. He was whistling softly.
> "Pachelbel," I said.
> He turned. "Huh? You talking to me?"
> "The canon by Pachelbel," I said. "It's what you were whistling. Can I talk to you for a minute?"

Major characters can—and should—be developed gradually. But writers need "tags"—quick, deft, unexpected strokes—to bring minor characters to life. A janitor who whistles classical tunes while he sweeps the floor, a beautiful actress who bites her fingernails, or a professor of Renaissance literature who carries a confession magazine under his arm, will etch themselves indelibly in your readers' memories.

These characters are established and ready to be more fully exploited if and when you choose.

Remember: In real life, we learn more about people through how they behave and talk than by how they look. How people appear, in fact, is often deceiving; the same is true of fictional characters. If you focus on your characters' speech, mannerisms, actions, and responses to situations in the story, you won't need to paint detailed physical descriptions of them or make them look strange for them to be memorable.

Avoid the trap of telling readers what to think about a character. Instead of calling a cab driver "grouchy," show him *acting* grouchy through what he says and how he behaves. Don't call a woman "flirtatious"; instead, show her flirting with a man.

Mystery readers want to figure it out for themselves, and they resent a writer's depriving them of the opportunity to draw their own conclusions about characters. The writer's golden rule—"Show don't tell"—is never more important than in creating interesting minor characters.

Secondary characters play a limited but crucial role in your story's development. You *needed* that whistling janitor to give your hero vital information, or to tell him the location of a businessman's office, or to direct him to the fire escape. He's a player. He might have a bit part, but without him the story will not work. He deserves your attention.

Some minor characters, of course, are simply walk-ons. They are the bus drivers, ushers, clerks, waitresses, and others who anonymously populate your story. They serve a function, and should be thought of as objects rather than characters. If a bartender's only function in your story is to deliver a drink, don't describe him or give him dialogue. Just call him "the bartender," as you'd call a passing vehicle "an automobile." Characterizing him further is not playing fair. It intrudes on your narrative and distorts it by suggesting that the bartender might be more significant than he really is.

Playing Mr. Potato Head

When my children were little, they had a toy called Mr. Potato Head. It came with plastic noses, ears, mouths, hats, moustaches, hairpieces, and glasses that they'd mix and match, sticking them onto a potato to create a face.

To create memorable minor characters, try playing Mr. Potato Head. Draw your characters from your experience. Mix and match the mannerisms, life experiences, and appearances of your friends and the people you encounter. Take note of how people around you act and react, speak and behave. Observe their table manners, reading habits, gestures, expressions. What do they watch on television? How do they spend their free time? What do they read, sing, and drink? How do they dress and wear their hair?

Don't seek bizarre combinations or you will create cartoons rather than believable characters. Encourage your reader to wonder about them and care about them. Don't present too much information; choose a few details, then allow your readers to use their imaginations to create their own interpretations.

Why, for example, does that actress bite her nails?

Did her parents mistreat her? Does her husband abuse her? Is she afraid or insecure or guilt-ridden?

Does the English professor with the confession magazine actually read it? Does he write confessions under a pen name? Is vital information coded into one of the magazine's stories?

And the janitor who whistles Pachelbel—were his parents classical music lovers? Was he—or is he—a serious musician? Did an accident, or an enemy, or a cruel trick of fate deprive him of a career as a concert violinist?

When a quick sketch prompts your readers to ask questions such as these, you've done your job.

≈ 5 ≈

Point of View: Giving Your Reader a Place to Stand

T HE NEXT TIME you find yourself in a crowded restaurant, take note of which sense impressions have registered on your consciousness. Perhaps you've tuned into the restrained argument between the young couple at the next table. Your waitress has a bawdy laugh and an engagement ring on her left hand. From the direction of the kitchen comes the aroma of sautéed garlic, which conjures up ancient memories of your grandmother's kitchen and reminds you that you skipped lunch.

Now ask your dinner companion what *she* notices. The Vivaldi they're piping in through the speakers is nice, she says, but the clank and clatter of silverware and crockery are terribly annoying. What about the waitress? Oh, she wears too much makeup and her roots are showing. The smell of garlic? Now that you mention it, it is a little unpleasant, isn't it?

You and your dining companion bring different memories, interests, sensitivities, moods, and expectations to the simple experience of sitting in a restaurant. Each of you notices different things. Your reconstruction of the evening is therefore radically different from that of your friend.

You can report it only as you experienced it—from your own point of view. That's why eyewitness accounts of events often conflict wildly with one another. For a great many reasons, all of us perceive and interpret things differently.

Of course, in reconstructing your evening at the restaurant you could also recount your dinner companion's impressions—but only as she chose to share them with you. You probably wouldn't know why she chose to be critical of the waitress's grooming or why she failed to notice the argument at the next table, although her facial expressions, gestures, tone of voice, and body language might give you clues. Perhaps she was jealous of the attentions the waitress received from her male customers. For all you know, your friend *was* eavesdropping but didn't want to admit it to you.

You experience your life only through your own point of view. Part of that experience, of course, comes through your interactions with others. But you can never crawl into other people's heads and experience what they experience, nor can you trust their reports to be entirely accurate or complete. People lie, distort, omit, and otherwise fail to say exactly what they really think. You must impose your interpretations on what others tell you, basing your conclusions both on what you know or infer about them and on your own preconceptions about human nature. In your interactions with others, you must rely on your own point of view.

In fiction, events are filtered through the five senses of the point-of-view characters and then reported to the reader. Establish your story's point of view immediately—preferably in the first sentence. Let your readers—the participants in your story's puzzle-solving quest—know whose shoes they will be walking in as they move through your story, whose eyes and ears and nose they'll be using to witness your story's events. Choosing your story's point of view is one of your most crucial storytelling decisions.

First person

The first-person narrator is the character who experiences the events of the story and who interprets and explains them to the reader in his or her own words.

Kinsey Millhone, for example, is the "I" in Sue Grafton's popular mystery series. Readers walk—and sometimes run—through the stories in Kinsey's shoes. They go only where she goes, know only what she knows, see and smell and hear only what she experiences and is aware of and believes is important. Readers don't know what any of the other characters is thinking or feeling or experiencing. They can only speculate based on what the characters say and how they act in Kinsey's presence.

Grafton begins *A Is for Alibi* by immediately establishing Kinsey's first-person narrative voice:

> My name is Kinsey Millhone. I'm a private investigator, licensed by the state of California. I'm thirty-two years old, twice divorced, no kids. The day before yesterday I killed someone and the fact weighs heavily on my mind.

The very first word in Grafton's book is that first-person possessive pronoun "my," clearly establishing the first-person point of view. Kinsey is straightforward and candid from the beginning. Readers trust she will tell them the truth, and they have faith that she will share important information with them.

Through the eyewitness reports of the first-person narrator, readers accumulate information. They test it, interpret it, link it with other bits of information, and formulate theories. Readers understand that things are happening offstage that Kinsey cannot tell us, and they assume that the story's other characters do not share all of their thoughts with her. Some characters, in fact, may mislead Kinsey. Others could be lying.

First-person narrators are not omniscient. As a young female California private investigator, Kinsey Millhone has her own ways of perceiving the world. She notices and understands things differently from the way John D. MacDonald's first-person narrator Travis McGee and Sara Paretsky's V. I. Warshawski do.

Readers who want to solve the case must take into account Kinsey's personality and limitations as well as the facts as she recounts them in her narrative.

It's no coincidence that so many successful mystery stories are told by first-person narrators. Readers readily identify with the "I" of these tales; it's a powerful alliance. If readers like and trust the first-person narrator, they feel that they have a friend. It makes for strong reader loyalty.

Readers meet and learn about other characters directly through the experiences and perceptions of the first-person narrator. For example, early in Linda Barnes's *A Trouble of Fools*, Carlotta Carlyle's doorbell rings:

It was slightly past noon on a late September Sunday that had no business being so cool, and I wasn't expecting anybody. I squinted my left eye shut and pressed my right one to the peephole. If I had been expecting someone, it wouldn't have been the cozy old lady who perched on my front stoop like an inquisitive bird. As I struggled with the last deadbolt, always sticky, she turned up the collar of her woolly pink coat, and got ready to hit the buzzer again. She wore white cotton gloves. I haven't seen a pair of white gloves in ages.

"Coming," I yelled, forestalling the buzzer.

She was too old for a Mormon missionary, so I steeled myself for the Jehovah's Witnesses pitch. Possibly Antivivisection. I hoped she was antivivisection. I wondered if I could keep a straight face while I asked her where to donate the parakeet for lab research.

She had sparse white hair, like powdered sugar frosting on her pink scalp, and a round face that must have been cheerful when she smiled. Her skin was crosshatched with fine lines. Deeper ridges creased her forehead and carved channels from her broad nose to her small anxious mouth. Her gray eyes, unsettlingly steady, stared gravely at the peephole.

The lock gave, and I yanked open the door, apologizing. She didn't respond like a proselytizer or a fundraiser.

"Margaret Devens," she announced hopefully. "Miss," she added. "Miss Margaret Devens, spinster."

In this passage, readers meet Margaret Devens through Carlotta's eyes, just as they might meet any person in real life. They form impressions based on what Carlotta observes and what Miss Devens chooses to say. Readers know only what Carlotta is thinking and feeling. They cannot enter Miss Devens's mind. The self-proclaimed spinster may subsequently prove to be a terrorist, or a kidnapper—or an antivivisectionist. But readers won't know that until Carlotta does.

Readers must respect the first-person narrator. She must be at least as intelligent and observant as they are if the puzzle-solving quest is to challenge both reader and narrator equally. Mystery readers do not want to solve the problem while the hero or heroine is still muddling around gathering clues and acting confused. First-person narration works best when the narrator is actively engaged in the story's quest. Give your sleuth reasons to go places, to witness events, and to have a variety of experiences. Her narration, as much as possible, should be firsthand and immediate. A passive sleuth such as Nero Wolfe (who rarely leaves his Manhattan apartment) would make a poor first-person narrator, as author Rex Stout realized. That's why Stout gave the narrating job to Archie Goodwin, Wolfe's gofer.

Suspense develops when narrators find themselves in trouble. They sometimes take risks, miscalculate, underestimate the danger of a situation, and confront a desperate adversary. Readers, identifying with the first-person narrator, accept her danger as their own.

But don't ever try to convince your readers that your first-person narrator might be killed. They know she survives. After all, she's lived to tell about it.

Third person limited

Closely related to the first-person point of view is the intimate, or limited, third-person narration. With the substitution of the third-person pronoun "he" or "she" for the first-person "I," the effect is almost identical. Readers identify only with the single viewpoint character. They know that that character—and only that character—is thinking and feeling and experiencing.

In her novel *The Sculptress*, Minette Walters introduces readers to Rosalind Leigh, the third-person narrator, as she awaits her prison interview with a convicted murderess:

> Rosalind Leigh, waiting by the door of the interview room, ran her tongue around the inside of her mouth. Her revulsion was immediate as if Olive's evil had reached out

and touched her. *My God*, she was thinking, and the thought alarmed her, *I can't go through with this*. But she had, of course, no choice. The gates of the prison were locked on her, as a visitor, just as securely as they were locked on the inmates. She pressed a shaking hand to her thigh where the muscles were jumping uncontrollably. Behind her, her all but empty briefcase, a testament to her lack of preparation for this meeting, screamed derision at her ill-considered assumption that conversation with Olivo could develop like any other. It had never occurred to her, not for one moment, that fear might stifle her inventiveness.

In this third-person passage, readers share the point-of-view character's thoughts and feelings just as intimately as if it were a first-person narration. The effect for readers is identical and equally powerful.

In the limited third-person narration, just as in first-person, readers meet secondary characters through the eyes of the point-of-view character. Here's how Thomas Harris, in *The Silence of the Lambs*, introduces Jack Crawford to readers through the point of view of Clarice Starling:

She found Jack Crawford alone in the cluttered suite of offices. He was standing at someone's else's desk talking on the telephone and she had a chance to look him over for the first time in a year. What she saw disturbed her.

Normally, Crawford looked like a fit, middle-aged engineer who might have paid his way through college playing baseball—a crafty catcher, tough when he blocked the plate. Now he was thin, his shirt collar was too big, and he had dark puffs under his reddened eyes. Everyone who could read the papers knew Behavioral Science section was catching hell. Starling hoped Crawford wasn't on the juice. That seemed most unlikely here.

In this passage, Harris manages to tell readers as much about Starling as about Crawford. Sharing her thoughts and feelings, readers learn that she is "disturbed." By her casual use of an analogy, readers know that she understands baseball. Her familiar reference to "Behavioral Science section" pegs her as an insider. She remembers how Crawford looked a year ago—a hint that they are acquaintances, but probably not close friends.

Harris scrupulously avoids telling us more about Crawford than Starling knows or observes. He thus does not violate the limitations of the intimate third-person narration.

When describing another character or an event through the third-person point of view, you might be tempted to step back and offer more information than the viewpoint character can know or observe. Don't do it. It's intrusive and confusing, and it destroys your reader's close identification with your point-of-view character.

Inattentive writers, for example, might construct a scene this way:

> Michael Blake took a deep breath and pushed open the glass door. He was worried, and a frown creased his handsome face. He saw Sarah Benjamin sitting at the patio table. Her glasses were perched low on her long aristocratic nose. She was reading some old letters from her missing daughter. She wore a bulky sweatshirt for warmth against the autumnal chill and an old pair of baggy blue jeans that had fit her snugly before the chemotherapy. Her ordeal had etched a few more wrinkles in her craggy face, but otherwise Blake thought she looked the same as ever.

Notice what happens here. The passage begins in Michael Blake's point of view (he "took a deep breath and pushed open the glass door"). Readers know his feelings (he "was worried"). So far, so good. But abruptly the eager writer intervenes to tell the reader that Blake frowns and that his face is handsome.

Think about it. When you frown, are you thinking of the expression on your face, or that it's "handsome"? No. You are thinking about whatever it is that causes you to frown. You would report what you see and how you feel—but *not* what your own face looks like. By describing Blake's face, the writer's own point of view takes over the scene, and the intimate third-person point of view has been destroyed.

Then readers are told that Sarah Benjamin is reading "old letters from her missing daughter." Can Blake see what she's reading from where he stands? Does he know who wrote them? No. The writer has intruded again. And then the writer proceeds to explain why Sarah is wearing a sweatshirt and even a bit of the history of her jeans—details which Blake, the ostensible viewpoint character, could not know.

Point-of-view violations such as these make readers feel schizophrenic. They become acutely aware of another point of view—that of the writer, who is manipulating these characters. Thus the intimate bond between the reader and the point-of-view character is broken.

A point-of-view trick

At the end of the first chapter of your mystery novel, your first-person narrator says: "I should never have answered the phone that night. I should have wrapped a pillow around my ears and let it ring. Little did I know that Chloe's seemingly innocent request would nearly cost me my life."

The transparent "little-did-I-know" foreshadowing trick is commonplace in first-person and limited third-person mystery stories. It seems to create suspense, saying, in effect, "Keep reading. There's an exciting story awaiting you."

Actually, unless the little-did-I-know device is used subtly and with restraint, readers will recognize it as a cheap trick. It betrays the insecurity of the writer who doesn't trust his own story to tug his readers forward. When the narrator says "little did I know," he is also saying, "Now I *do* know, but I'm not going to tell you yet. You've got to read this book to find out." Thus the narrator is admitting that he does not intend to be entirely candid with the reader, and the strong narrator-reader bond of trust is weakened.

A variation on the "little-did-I-know" trick occurs when the narrator introduces a piece of evidence and then refuses to describe it to the reader for several pages. For example: "Between the pages of the old family Bible I found an envelope. With shaking hands, I tore it open and slid out a single piece of paper. I read it slowly. Then I sat down, lit a cigarette, and read it again. I felt beads of sweat form on my forehead."

At this point, of course, the reader expects to be told what is written on that piece of paper. The narrator knows, and the reader trusts her.

But instead, the scene continues: "I folded the paper thoughtfully and slipped it into my purse. It answered a lot of questions. I stood up, stubbed out my cigarette in the heavy glass ashtray, and went to the telephone. It was time to talk to Charles."

By now, the frustrated reader is asking: When is she going to tell me what's written on that piece of paper?

The writer is trying to create suspense, and it's a valid technique *provided it's done with restraint*. For example, readers will not object if the point-of-view character reads the note to Charles over the telephone. But if she has a conversation with Charles in which she still fails to divulge the contents of the paper, and if she then gets into her car, drives to her lawyer's house, has a discussion with him, and proceeds to confront several other characters, and *still* does not explain what's written on that all-important piece of paper, readers will begin to feel betrayed by this point-of-view character whom they've trusted. They will resent her coyness. She has key information that she's not sharing, and readers will correctly feel that she has violated the mystery story's rule of fair play.

Multiple point of view

In the suspense stories of writers such as Barbara Michaels and Ken Follett, the whodunit puzzle, if it exists at all, is usually secondary. The question that propels the plots of suspense novels typically asks: Will the good guy succeed in preventing the bad guy from completing his evil plan?

Suspense stories, thrillers, and other mystery subgenres derive their tension less from a puzzle than from the uncertainty of the outcome. There's a contest between good and evil, and readers follow the play of both sides. They turn the pages to find out who wins.

Sooner or later, readers generally learn who the villain of a suspense story is. As often as not they spend time in his or her point of view. The question is not the villain's identity or motivation. Rather, the problem that drives the suspense plot is whether this villain will succeed in his plan to assassinate the President, or blow up the chemical factory, or kill more archeology students. Will the heroine stop him in the nick of time? Will she manage to find out where the kidnapped child is being hidden before the bomb explodes? Will the villain kill the heroine's brother?

Suspense can be enhanced by alternating the narration among the points of view of several different characters. In *The Silence of the Lambs*, for example, readers witness most of the scenes from Clarice Starling's viewpoint. But Harris heightens the suspense of his story by periodically showing scenes from the point of view of other characters, including the victims, the evil Dr. Lector, and Jame Gumb, the story's villain.

If you're writing a mystery story in which the central quest involves solving a puzzle, however, stick with a single point of view. First person or third person. Your choice. Don't be tempted to tell your reader what your other characters are thinking and feeling by entering their viewpoints. That will divide your readers' attention and blur their identification with your sleuth.

There are, of course, exceptions. Tony Hillerman, for example, masterfully alternates between two intimate third-person points of view in his mystery novels. But Hillerman *is* a master, and his series features two more or less equal protagonists, Joe Leaphorn and Jim Chee. Most successful mystery writers, however, stick to the single point of view. Beginners should do the same.

Besides blurring your readers' identification with your sleuth, the multiple viewpoint also creates tactical problems in puzzle-driven mystery fiction. When writers alternate point of view among several characters, readers inevitably know more than the story's sleuth. They have the advantage over her, which violates the rule of fair play just as surely as if vital information were withheld from readers.

Here, for example, is a scene as it might be told from a secondary character's viewpoint (Sarah Benjamin) rather than the story's sleuth (Michael Blake):

> Sarah peered over the tops of her glasses and watched Michael push open the glass door and step tentatively onto

the patio. She saw a frown crease his handsome face. Poor Michael, she thought. He was a nice guy, but he didn't know any more about how to deal with a dying old woman than anyone else.

She shivered. Even in her bulky sweatshirt, she was cold. She was always cold. The chemotherapy had sucked all the warmth from her body. In spite of what the doctors told her, she knew she'd never be warm again.

Or perhaps it was rereading Mary Ann's old letters that gave her the chills.

Well, maybe Michael would help. She hoped so. She didn't know where else to turn.

He'd resist, she expected. He'd protest that he was a lawyer, not a private eye, that he was overworked as it was. Dear Michael. She knew that he'd rather go golfing. She'd have to handle him carefully.

Here readers know things about Sarah that Michael, the sleuth, can only surmise. Through Sarah's point of view readers learn that she intends to "handle him carefully." They know that she will attempt to manipulate him. Michael, at best, can only deduce this important fact.

At this point in the story, readers might legitimately consider Sarah a suspect. Once they hear her thoughts and share her feelings, however, they *know* that she should be deleted from their list of suspects, because if she had committed the murder, it's reasonable to assume that she would be thinking about it. Readers are disappointed that the complexity of the mystery is thus reduced.

Suppose Sarah actually *is* the villain?

Writers who enter the point of view of the villain either cheat inexcusably or give the puzzle's solution away. Fair play demands that no point-of-view character can lie to readers, or deceive them, or withhold crucial information from them. Obviously, uppermost in the murderer's mind are that he did the deed, that he desperately wants to get away with it, and that people are trying to bring him to justice.

To have him *not* think these thoughts is cheating your reader. On the other hand, if he *does* share these thoughts with readers, they will solve the mystery puzzle before your sleuth does.

Writing in the point of view of all significant characters *except* the villain will also give away the mystery of observant readers. They will notice whose point of view you are avoiding, and they will figure out why.

Omniscient point of view

The omniscient narrator is the author himself, who knows everything and who shares—and withholds—information from the reader as she chooses. This kind of narration, unless handled with great care, feels arbitrary to readers. They tend to feel manipulated by it. They know they are being told only what the writer chooses to tell them. The puzzle feels like a game of hide-and-seek between writer and reader, rather than a problem for the reader to share with a sympathetic sleuth.

Here is a version of our earlier scene between Michael Blake and Sarah Benjamin, this time told from the point of view of an omniscient narrator:

An anxious smile creased Michael Blake's handsome face. The tall, middle-aged lawyer pushed open the glass door. He was wearing a pin-striped suit. A thin leather briefcase dangled from his hand. He looked at the old woman sitting at the patio table. Her glasses were perched low on her long aristocratic nose. She was reading old letters from her daughter. Sarah Benjamin hadn't seen Mary Ann since the

death of her husband, Mary Ann's father. All she had left
were these faded old letters.

Blake was not only Sarah's lawyer. He was also her friend
and confidant. He wasn't sure why she had summoned him.
He knew she was dying of cancer. Probably she wanted to
straighten out her will, settle things while she was still able.

"Sarah," he said to her, making his voice as gentle and
friendly as he could under the circumstances.

When she heard Michael's voice, Sarah peered up at him
over the tops of her glasses. She shivered. In spite of the
bulky sweatshirt—it had once belonged to Mary Ann, a
souvenir from their summer trip to Quebec back when
Charles was still alive—she was cold. It was the damned
chemotherapy.

With this omniscient narration, the reader wanders
more or less randomly into and out of the heads of the
two characters. Sometimes they are seen from a distance
as they are described by the author. At other times the
reader is privy to their thoughts. Readers are given no
shoes to stand in except those of the all-knowing writer,
and they are being asked to identify with two characters
simultaneously.

Except in highly skilled hands, omniscient narration
feels manipulative and impersonal. Even when it manages to sustain a complex puzzle, it discourages readers
from caring about it or trying to solve it.

The neutral or missing point of view

A variation of the omniscient is the point of view that
consistently keeps readers at arm's length from all the
story's characters. The all-seeing narrator reports only
what is observable and refrains from entering any character's mind.

The neutral narrator reports the Michael Blake-Sarah
Benjamin scene this way:

Michael Blake pushed open the glass door. Sarah Benjamin was sitting at the patio table. Her glasses were perched low on her long aristocratic nose. She was studying a stack of papers. She wore a bulky sweatshirt and baggy blue jeans. There were deep creases in her craggy face.

"Sarah," said Blake gently.

She raised her eyes over her glasses without lifting her head. "Well, hello, Michael," she said with a soft smile. "Come sit."

He went over and sat across from her. She held her bony hand to him and he took it.

"You've been avoiding me," she said.

"Nonsense," he replied.

In this example, the creases in Sarah's face and her bony hand simply describe her. They no longer work to hint at Michael's fondness for Sarah or his concern about her deteriorating health.

Unlike the omniscient, the neutral point of view is really no point of view at all. Because it forces readers to observe each character through a one-way mirror and prevents them from entering any character's mind, they are unlikely to care deeply about any of them.

Second person point of view

In the second person, the narrator is someone called "you." Instead of a character being the story's protagonist and narrator, "you" are.

For example:

You take a deep breath and push open the door. You see Sarah sitting at the patio table. She's not looking well, you think.

"Sarah," you say.

With this point of view, you hope to convince your reader to become a character in your story. But readers *know* they're not pushing open doors and speaking to Sarah.

Avoid the second-person point of view, if only because it's so unusual that it calls attention to itself. It strikes the reader as a facile stylistic trick. To be effective, writing should be invisible. It should allow readers to submerge themselves in the story by identifying with a single sympathetic character. Second-person narration keeps reminding readers that they're being toyed with by a writer who's trying awfully hard to be clever. It gives them *no* character to connect with.

A short story might sustain a second-person narrator. But I know of no mystery novel that's done it successfully—or of any serious writers who'll admit that they've even tried.

≈ 6 ≈
Setting: The Scene of the Crime

N0 MATTER WHAT your sleuth is doing—driving a car through the night, interviewing a suspect, waiting in an office, getting beaten up, watching television, or lying in bed thinking—she always has to be somewhere.

You can't have a scene without a setting.

Setting is more than place

Setting is more than geographical place. It comprises all the conditions under which things happen—region, neighborhood, buildings, interiors, climate, weather, topography, flora, fauna, time of day, season of year. It involves not just the scenery, but also the sounds and smells and textures of places.

Successful mysteries have been set in every imaginable city and region in the world. Big cities such as New York, London, Boston, Detroit, and Los Angeles are popular. Sara Paretsky has put Chicago on the mystery map. But increasingly such writers as Tony Hillerman and Jake Page are invoking the richness of the American Southwest. Carl Hiaasen and Edna Buchanan are among the many who set their mysteries in Florida. Dana Sabenow writes about Alaska and Patricia Cornwell about Richmond, Virginia. Philip R. Craig's novels take place on Martha's Vineyard; Brendan DuBois writes about New Hampshire's few miles of seashore. All of these settings work because the authors *know* them. What's really important is being so familiar with your settings that you can invoke the defining details that will bring them to life and be useful in your stories.

Your settings must strike your readers as realistic. A true-to-life setting persuades readers to suspend their disbelief and accept the premise that your story really happened. The easiest way to do this is to write knowledgeably and confidently about real places.

Mood, theme, and character

Mystery writers appeal to all of their readers' senses to establish their story's setting and mood. James Lee Burke, in *Black Cherry Blues*, evokes a section of Baton Rouge this way:

> . . . The rain clattered on my truck cab, and the wind was blowing strong out of the southwest, across the Atchafalaya swamp, whipping the palm and oak trees by the highway. West Baton Rouge, which begins at the Mississippi River, has always been a seedy area of truck stops, marginal gambling joints, Negro and blue-collar bars. To the east you can see the lighted girders of the Earl K. Long Bridge, plumes of smoke rising from the oil refineries, the state capitol building silhouetted in the rain. Baton Rouge is a green town full of oak trees, parks, and lakes, and the thousands of lights on the refineries and chemical plants are regarded as a testimony to financial security rather than a sign of industrial blight. But once you drive west across the metal grid of the bridge and thump down on the old cracked four-lane, you're in a world that caters to the people of the

> Atchafalaya basin—Cajuns, redbones, roustabouts, pipe-liners, rednecks whose shrinking piece of American geography is identified only by a battered pickup, a tape deck playing Waylon, and a twelve-pack of Jax.

In this passage, Burke's narrator focuses on his physical surroundings—the colors and sounds and the people who are part of the place. Although Burke does not directly describe any sense impressions other than "clattered" and "thump," it's easy to smell the refineries and chemical plants and to feel the dampness of the southwest wind that blows in from the swamp.

In a film or a stage play, the setting is always visible to the viewer, and conversations, actions and setting are available simultaneously. Complex settings do not distract from other components of the scene. In a book or short story, however, all that's visible is what the writer presents in words. A powerful paragraph of description such as Burke's does not interrupt the story's flow. Longer—or less adept—descriptive passages, on the other hand, can cause readers to lose touch with the story's characters and action.

The writer's challenge is to integrate setting into a scene's other components, such as dialogue and action, so that it is vivid without interrupting or intruding on the events. Here is how Sue Grafton's narrator, Kinsey Millhone, describes the motel she has just entered, in *F Is for Fugitive*:

> I moved to the counter and peered to my right. Through an open door, I caught a glimpse of a hospital bed. There was the murmur of voices, but I couldn't see a soul. I heard the muffled flushing of a toilet, pipes clanking noisily. The air was soon scented with the artificial bouquet of room spray, impossibly sweet. Nothing in nature has ever smelled like that.

Several minutes passed. There was no seating available, so I stood where I was, turning to survey the narrow room. . . .

Here the descriptions are short, so that the reader's attention remains on Kinsey. The smells and sounds of the motel are carefully woven into the scene without distracting readers from their focus on Kinsey and her reason for being there.

Opening scenes with setting

Films typically begin with an "establishing shot." The camera pans across a crowded restaurant or a mountain range or a city street to fix the viewer in a place *before the action begins.* Coming at the beginning, establishing shots do not interrupt ongoing action or distract the viewer.

Mystery writers can use the establishing shot to equally good effect. The following passage, for example, begins Chapter One in Peter Hoeg's *Smilla's Sense of Snow:*

It's freezing—an extraordinary 0-degree Fahrenheit— and it's snowing, and in the language that is no longer mine, the snow is *ganik*—big, almost weightless crystals falling in clumps and covering the ground with a layer of pulverized white frost.

December, darkness rises up from the grave, seeming as limitless as the sky above us. In this darkness our faces are merely pale, shining orbs . . .

Here Hoeg uses an establishing shot of the dominant element in the setting, the snow. Then he pans quickly to the cemetery ("the grave") before establishing that other people ("our faces") are present in the scene.

Lawrence Sanders begins *The First Deadly Sin* this way:

> There was quiet. He lay on his back atop a shaft of stone called Devil's Needle, and felt he was lost, floating in air. Above him, all about him stretched a thin blue sac. Through it he could see scribbles of clouds, a lemon sun.
>
> He heard nothing but his own strong heart, the slowly quieting of his breath as he recovered from his climb. He could believe he was alone in the universe.
>
> Finally, he stood and looked around him. Waves of foliage lapped at the base of his stone; it was a dark green ocean with a froth of autumn's russet. He could see the highway, the tarred roofs of Chilton, a steel ribbon of river uncoiling southward to the sea.

Sanders's opening scene, like Hoeg's, depends largely on description. But neither of the scenes is static. Something is happening. In Hoeg's beginning, the narrator's distinctive observations, plus her use of an unusual foreign word, draws readers into the story that will unfold. In the scene by Sanders, readers are acutely aware that the scenery is being presented through the eyes of the point-of-view character, who has just climbed to the top of this rock. Besides establishing specific seasons and locations, both scenes introduce readers to the characters' narrative voices and, by their observations, give hints about their personalities and interests. The two scenes also establish certain expectations in the reader and set the tone for what follows. In this way, even relatively straightforward narrative descriptions, when presented through the point of view of the protagonist, can serve many purposes.

It's not a good idea to postpone the action until you've set the stage in *every* scene. You might want to open with a snatch of dialogue or a glimpse of a character.

But you must quickly give the reader a sense of where and when the scene is occurring. You can integrate a fuller description of the setting into the action of the scene later, so that the separate parts of the scene work together unobtrusively.

Here, for example, is the way Eileen Dreyer begins the prologue to her novel *A Man to Die For:*

> Control your impulses, her mother had always said. Stifle your urges, the church echoed. She should have listened. The next time she had an urge like this one, she was going to lock herself in a closet until it went away.
>
> "Honey, why are we here?"
>
> "I have to make a stop before I take you home, Mom."
>
> A stop. She had to report a crime. Several crimes. That wasn't exactly a run to the local Safeway for deodorant.
>
> Gripping her purse in one hand and her mother in the other, Casey McDonough approached the St. Louis City Police Headquarters like a penitent approaching the gates of purgatory. It seemed amazing, really. Casey had been born no more than fifteen miles away, but she'd never visited this place before. She'd never even known precisely where it was.
>
> A stark block of granite that took up the corner of Clark and Tucker, the headquarters did nothing to inspire comfort. Brass grillwork protected massive front doors and encased traditional globe lamps that flanked it. . . .

In this opener, Dreyer uses four short paragraphs to introduce two characters and to create a feeling of urgency before letting readers know where the scene takes place. Delaying significantly longer could risk making readers feel disoriented.

Making settings authentic

You *must* get actual places precisely right. One sour note and you risk losing your reader's trust.

A friend once recommended that I read a book that was set in Boston. In the first chapter was a reference to Newbury Street—except it was spelled N-e-w-b-e-r-r-y. This writer can't be trusted even to get place names right, I thought. How can I believe this story?

I closed the book and didn't pick it up again.

Making settings absolutely authentic requires research. No matter how many times you've been there, it's a good idea to go back to the places you intend to write about. Observe the people, listen to the sounds, sniff the smells, absorb the colors and textures, talk with the people you meet. Note the vivid images that define the place. Look for the striking details that make it unique and distinctive and that will enable you to bring it to life for your readers.

Here's how Patricia Cornwell leads her readers into a morgue in *Cruel and Unusual:*

> Inside the morgue, fluorescent light bleached the corridor of color, the smell of deodorizer cloying. I passed the small office where funeral homes signed in bodies, then the X-ray room, and the refrigerator, which was really a large refrigerated room with double-decker gurneys and two massive steel doors. The autopsy suite was lit up, stainless steel tables polished bright. Susan was sharpening a long knife and Fielding was labeling blood tubes. Both of them looked as tired and unenthusiastic as I felt.

Visiting your local morgue may not be your idea of fun. But it's necessary if you want to describe it with the authority that Cornwell does here. Don't rely on your imagination or what you've seen on television to give you the telling details or the smells and sounds of a place. If it's worth writing about at all, it's worth getting absolutely right.

In many cases, researching settings is not unpleasant.

For example, you should make it a point to eat in every restaurant you write about, no matter how familiar it already is to you, at least twice—once just before writing the scene to fix it in your mind, and once again afterwards to make sure you've gotten it right. This is not hard work.

Invented settings

Don't feel limited to using actual places if doing so will alter the story you want to tell. An invented setting can still ring true for your readers. Ed McBain fabricated the 87th Precinct and the city where it lies. Katherine Hall Page invented the Massachusetts town of Aleford, and Sue Grafton's Santa Teresa is a fictional place, too. Those who write about actual places commonly invent restaurants, businesses, and residences in them. Readers will readily accept the invented places as real provided they resemble actual places.

If the setting you need exists, use it; if it doesn't exist, make it up, but make it true.

Milieu

In addition to all of the physical elements of place, setting includes the cultures and professions and other activities of your characters. Horse racing lore is as much a part of Dick Francis's novels as the racetracks themselves. Forensic medicine is a vital part of the settings in Patricia Cornwell's stories. Police procedure is integral to the settings in the works of William Caunitz, Joseph Wambaugh, Ed McBain, and other writers whose main characters are police officers. Sports such as professional baseball and college basketball have served as background for novels by Robert Parker. The traditions and ceremonies of the Navajos are important in the reservation settings in Tony Hillerman's stories.

A setting can be another historical time. Steven Saylor's short stories, for example, take place in Caesar's Rome. Ellis Peters's Brother Cadfael novels are set in medieval Europe. Carole Nelson Douglas, among others, writes Sherlock Holmes pastiches set in Victorian London. Max Allan Collins's Nathan Heller series revisits famous American crimes. Robert K. Tanenbaum's Butch Karp, New York City Assistant District Attorney, works in the 1970s. In all cases, the stories are convincing because the authors exhaustively research the historical period they've chosen to write about. A single mistake in the customs, technology, speech patterns, or dress of the times can destroy the willingness of knowledgeable readers to believe your story.

An authentic milieu helps convince readers that your story is real. It can also appeal to readers' curiosity. Everybody likes to learn something new, and when readers can learn while they're absorbed by an entertaining mystery story, they like it even better.

Settings that work overtime

Your setting is more than just a backdrop for the action of your story. The conditions under which the action occurs can actually do double or even triple duty for you. Setting creates mood and tone. The places where characters live and work give clues to their personalities and motivations. Place, weather, climate, season of year, and time of day can cause things to happen in a story just as surely as characters can.

Shakespeare and Conan Doyle understood how setting can establish mood and foreshadow events. The "dark and stormy night" had its purpose, as did the spooky mansion on the remote moor or the thick fog of a London evening. Contemporary writers use thunderstorms and abandoned warehouses and barrooms and the back alleys of city slums in the same way.

Modern readers are sophisticated, however, and writers have to keep up with them. Obvious settings can too easily become literary clichés. If you misuse or overuse them, they lose their punch.

Never underestimate the power of going against stereotypes. Seek subtlety and irony. Murder can be committed anywhere, anytime. When it happens on a sunny May morning in a suburban backyard, for example, or in a church or school or hospital, the horror of it is intensified.

Carefully selected details of setting delineate the characters who populate it. The pictures or calendars that hang on the office wall suggest the interests and personality of the person who works there. Look for the small details that tell readers about a character before they even see him or her: a policeman's desk littered with half-empty styrofoam coffee cups or cigar butts or used tea bags or chewing gum wrappers; the absence of a family portrait on the desk of a corporate CEO; the music that's played on a lawyer's phone line while your protagonist is on hold; a week's worth of newspapers piled on an elderly widow's front porch; a specimen jar containing a smoker's lung sitting on the desk of a forensic pathologist; a bag of golf clubs in the corner of a politician's office; or, a stack of old *Field & Stream* magazines on the table in a dentist's waiting room.

In *Billingsgate Shoal* Rick Boyer's oral surgeon protagonist, Doc Adams, visits his friend Moe Abramson:

> Soon I was reclining in a two-thousand-dollar belting leather Eames chair, watching the thirty-gallon aquarium. Two cardinal tetras chased each other from territory to territory. Small iridescent schools of neon tetras and zebra

dianos winked about under the fluorescent light. A Mozart concerto hummed and danced in the background.

An office featuring a big aquarium and Mozart's music can reveal as much about a character—even before you meet him—as his dress, manner of speech, or physical appearance.

Compare what Moe Abramson's office reveals about him with what you might deduce about the man whose apartment Carlotta Carlyle enters in Linda Barnes's *A Trouble of Fools:*

> . . . I breathed in a considerable amount of air and was surprised to find it sweet. The place was clean. Pat's flat was a shabby affair, Spartan, the final resting place of a fussy old flirtatious bachelor. Probably a virgin. A faded print couch anchored one wall. Blowsy off-white curtains framed the windows. A framed picture of Jesus hung on the wall over the sofa, a crucifix next to it. A threadbare easy chair with a fat dented cushion faced off against a huge color TV. The furniture wasn't arranged with conversational groupings in mind. It was set up for one man watching TV alone.

The secret of a successfully rendered setting lies *not* in piling detail upon detail. Boyer highlights just three details of Moe Abramson's office—the Eames chair, the aquarium, and the Mozart concerto. Barnes focuses on the furnishings in Pat's apartment. And yet in both cases a few carefully chosen details enable readers to color in these settings from their own imaginations.

Think of your settings as characters in your stories. Settings need not be passive; they can act and interact with your characters. Rainstorms cause automobile accidents. Snowstorms cover footprints and stall traffic. The bitter cold of winter kills homeless people in a city park.

Water released from a dam raises the level in a river and drowns a trout fisherman.

As you plan your stories, your setting may, at first, be vague and arbitrary. The storyline usually comes first, since it involves character, conflict, motive, detection, and resolution. But as the story begins to grow in your imagination, you'll discover that you need to place it somewhere specific, and as that happens, you'll think of ways that the various elements of setting—place, weather, time of year, and so forth—can give your plot its distinctiveness.

For the general storyline, it may be enough to know that a dead body must be found in Chapter One. Once you decide where your tale will take place, however, you should spend time there. Search out particular places where the events in your story can occur. Visit them often enough to absorb their sounds and smells, their colors, their details. Hang around. Talk to the local people. Walk up the alleys.

Learning the skills of observation will make you a better writer. Look at the places you visit through the lens of a camera. Photographs will help jar your imagination when you're at your typewriter or word processor. If you have an artistic bent, make sketches. Carry a tape recorder and record your observations.

As many details as you gather for your setting, however, avoid extended descriptive passages, because no matter how poetic and original you make them, and no matter how much you might admire the elegance of your own prose, these kinds of passages risk becoming self-indulgent. If they're too long, they will stall the momentum of the action and threaten to bore your reader, who is eager for the story to continue.

The key to creating effective settings in mystery fiction lies in finding the few *telling* details that will hint at all of the others. Be spare and suggestive. Look for a water stain on the ceiling or a cigarette burn on the sofa. Note the odor of mildew or the rattle of a loose windowpane. If you find the right details, your readers will draw the conclusions you want them to without losing track of the story itself.

≈ 7 ≈

Getting It Started: Setting the Narrative Hook

THE NEXT TIME you visit a bookstore, do what most fiction writers do in public settings: Watch the people. Find a browser and study the way she selects a book to purchase.

Something compels her to pull a book from the shelf. Perhaps it's the color of the jacket, or a familiar author's name on the spine. Maybe it's an intriguing title. Whatever her reasons, she now holds a book in her hands. She examines the front cover. That may be enough to cause her to replace the book and choose another.

But if she continues to hold onto that book, she probably flips it over and looks at the back of the jacket. If the author's picture or the blurbs that scream "Amazing!" "Irresistible!" "A real page-turner!" don't put her off, she opens the book and reads the "flap copy," which is generally a plot summary designed as a come-on.

So far, all of the bookselling work has been done by the publisher (except possibly the creation of the title, although publishers often reject the writer's title if they don't think it will grab that browser's attention). Of course, if the author has been published before, his or her name alone might be enough to sell the book.

Potential buyers, at least initially, really do judge books by their covers.

But they do not fork over credit cards for book covers. Watch your browser. If she's still holding that book, she'll next turn to the first page, *and she'll start reading.* This is the writer's moment of truth. Now that potential book buyer is judging the author's work. Keep watching her. Does she quickly shut the book and replace it on the shelf? Or does she lean against the wall and turn a page or two, then smile and sigh and tuck the book under her arm? If so, she's hooked.

Editors and agents evaluate manuscripts the same way that browsers evaluate published books. They read the first sentence, fully prepared to stop there. They believe that a dull or awkward or confusing first sentence portends a dull or awkward or confusing book. But if they're not discouraged, they'll read the entire first paragraph—again, perfectly willing to reject that manuscript if they aren't moved to keep reading.

An opening that compels editors—and book buyers—to continue turning the pages is *absolutely essential* for the unknown writer who wants to be published. It's not enough, of course. A good beginning does not make a good book or guarantee a sale.

But the converse can be considered a truth: A bad start virtually guarantees rejection.

The narrative hook

Opening a book is like meeting a stranger. The first impression makes all the difference. How do the first lines greet the reader? Do they smile softly and seductively? Do they open a trap door and drop the reader into a strange and mysterious new place, or do they crack open a window shade and offer a glimpse? Do they charm readers with their wit? Do they reach out and grab the reader by the throat, or do they politely take the reader's hand and invite her to join them? Do they scream of danger and mystery, or do they enfold the reader in a warm and comforting embrace?

Opening lines can be inviting and irresistible; they can also be awkward, offensive, or dull. They are the window to the book's personality. If the book's beginning doesn't hook readers, they will not read on.

Not any old hook will do. Dramatic, stylized, or otherwise attention-grabbing beginnings are effective *only if they draw your reader into the story.* That's why it's called a *narrative* hook.

An effective narrative hook promises a compelling story populated with fascinating characters. You've got only a few sentences—a couple of paragraphs at the most—to make that promise.

Many different kinds of narrative hooks are available to the mystery writer:

1. *The middle of a scene.* The classical device of beginning *in medias res* (in the middle of things), when executed effectively, drops readers into a situation. They will want to read on to discover both how that situation developed and how it resolves itself. By then they will be hooked on the story.

For example, here is how Ed McBain begins *Ghosts*:

> They might have been ghosts themselves, the detectives who stood in the falling snow around the body of the woman on the sidewalk. Shrouded by the swirling flakes, standing in snow three inches deep underfoot, they huddled like uncertain specters against the gray facade of the apartment building behind the slain woman.

Who is this dead woman? What happened to her? Who are the detectives? Can they uncover the mystery of her death? Such questions are implicit in these two opening sentences. The trap door has opened and readers have fallen in. They will read on.

2. *A vivid glimpse of setting.* Readers are generally fascinated with places. A memorable picture of a place will pull readers into the narrative.

In *Billingsgate Shoal*, Rick Boyer's Doc Adams greets his readers:

> Two and a half miles directly offshore from our cottage in Eastham, Massachusetts on Cape Cod, lies Billingsgate Shoal. It appears on nautical charts in a color between that of either land or sea. This is because Billingsgate is a sunken island and is visible only briefly, in all its soggy splendor, twice a day at tide's farthest ebb.

These opening sentences give readers a peek at a place they'd like to know better. The lines work because readers are confident that the narrator knows exactly what he is talking about. The details are precise and specific and absolutely true. Readers feel they are in good hands, and they also believe that the place Doc Adams describes has relevance to the story that will follow. Billingsgate Shoal seems like a vaguely mysterious place. Things can happen there.

Also important is the early signpost that a character has engaged the reader in a conversation. With the phrase "our cottage," Boyer establishes his first-person point of view in the first sentence. So in this brief, rather straightforward descriptive beginning, a great deal is promised. Readers want to hear more.

3. *A tidbit of interesting information.* Tell readers something they probably don't know, and promise them that this information will be relevant to the story that follows. Readers love to learn new things from novels. Here is an example from my novel, *The Spotted Cats:*

In Zambia the leopard is called *Nyalubwe*. In East Africa the natives call him *Chui*, and farther south he's called *Ingwe*. But everywhere—in Africa, in Asia, in parts of Europe and the Middle East—the leopard is the same animal: a perfect killing machine, the most efficient mammal predator—aside from man—on earth.

This kind of beginning works best when the information is both specific and arcane. Don't tell readers what many of them are already likely to know. The informational opening succeeds when the information itself hints at danger or mystery *and* the narrative voice is confident.

4. *A snatch of dialogue.* Dialogue is immediate. Stories that open with dialogue accomplish several things at once: They introduce the point-of-view character and at least one other; they create an *in medias res* sense that the reader has entered an ongoing scene; they suggest conflict and hint at mystery and drama; and they characterize the players by what they say and how they speak.

Blanche on the Lam, Barbara Neely's Agatha Award-winning first novel, begins this way:

> "Have you anything to say for yourself?" The judge gave Blanche a look that made her raise her handbag to her chest like a shield.
>
> "Your Honor . . . I'm sorry. . . . I . . ."
>
> "Sorry? It most certainly is sorry! This is the fourth, I repeat, the fourth, time that you've been before this court on a bad-check charge. Perhaps some time in a jail cell will convince you to earn your money before you spend it, like the rest of us. Thirty days and restitution!"

In this brief conversational exchange, Neely creates two characters and establishes a problem. It's an efficient and compelling way to begin a book.

5. *A dramatic moment.* Begin at the beginning—the precise moment when the puzzle presents itself. If it happens suddenly, and if its implications are powerful, you will instantly hook your readers.

Here, for example, in the single compelling opening sentence of *Darker than Amber,* John D. MacDonald grabs his readers' attention:

> We were about to give up and call it a night when somebody dropped the girl off the bridge.

Similarly, Edna Buchanan begins *Contents Under Pressure* this way:

> I stopped to listen. So did a detective and several patrolmen, frozen in motion. One cocked his head and held his walkie up to his ear. The morning had started out as a slow news day, but that could change in a heartbeat. It was happening now.

What happens next? Readers will feel compelled to find out.

6. *An appealing narrative voice.* You don't need high drama or clever wordplay or other tricks to capture your readers' interest. Promise them that they'll be keeping good company on their journey through your story, and they'll want to keep reading.

Here, in *A Beautiful Place to Die,* Philip R. Craig's Martha's Vineyard detective J. W. Jackson invites readers to join him:

> The alarm went off at three-thirty. Outside it was as black as a tax collector's heart. Smart me had stopped at the market the night before for doughnuts, so I was on the road as soon as I filled my thermos with coffee. I rattled through Edgartown without seeing another soul and went

on south toward Katama. The air was sharp and dry, and the wind was light from the southwest. Maybe it would blow the bluefish in at last. They were two weeks late, or at least two weeks later than the year before. The heater in the Landcruiser didn't work too well, so I was a bit chilly for the first few miles.

It's a quiet, confident, friendly beginning. Jackson, the narrator, is not out to impress us. Come along, he seems to say. Sit here beside me in my Landcruiser. I expect we'll have some fun.

The most dramatic question raised in this opening paragraph is whether the bluefish will be in. There is no hint of danger, no puzzle, no apparent conflict or tension. And yet Craig's straightforward prose lures readers into his story. Readers can't help liking this narrator and his down-to-earth attention to doughnuts and coffee and his car's heater. They look forward to spending more time with him. They are hooked.

The promise of the narrative hook

The simple job of your story's first sentence is to persuade your readers to read the second sentence, which will lead them to the third, and so on. But no matter how catchy, the beginning of your story will fail unless it fulfills the promises it makes to your readers.

In every opening you make implicit promises to your readers that:

1. Events described in the first scene are relevant to the story that follows.

2. Characters who appear in the opening are significant players in the story.

3. The mood created in the beginning foreshadows events to come.

4. The narrative voice will sustain itself all the way to the end.

5. Conflicts hinted at early will be resolved as the story develops.

6. Themes established at the beginning will be expanded and explored through the story's events and characters.

A flashy, attention-getting opening that fails to fulfill these promises can make readers feel deceived and cheated. Don't promise what you cannot or do not intend to deliver.

Remember: It's not any old hook. It's a *narrative* hook. The job of the opening is to lure readers into your story. After that, the story must do its own work.

Begin at the beginning—not before

Commonly, inexperienced writers feel compelled to begin their stories with reams of background information. They feel they must share those character biographies they worked so hard to create, or they compose detailed summaries of the events that preceded the story itself. They write long descriptions of setting or some aimless dialogue that is intended to help readers "get to know" the characters.

The story itself may finally get underway in the second or third chapter. But readers may not be there to enjoy it. One of the surest ways to bore readers and cause them to stop reading is to tell them what they don't have any reason to want to know.

You may need to warm up by writing your way to your story's actual beginning. Fine. Do it. Just be sure to delete it once you find the place where your story really starts.

Stories should open at a significant moment. Begin with *characters in meaningful situations*. Readers do not need to know who the characters are, where they came from, what happened to them earlier, or what they want. Readers don't yet care about your characters' previous lives, and they don't need an explanation of what's going on. Not yet.

Never give readers information before they want it. If your opening scene introduces compelling characters in conflict, readers will read on to learn more about them. The promise of fuller understanding is a powerful hook.

Begin at the beginning. Never earlier.

≈ 8 ≈

Structuring the Story: Building Tension

YOU'VE DONE ALL your preliminary work. You've come up with an original idea; your characters live in your imagination; you've decided on a point of view; you've found a vivid setting; and you've sketched out key scenes.

Now it's time to assemble these elements into a plot.

Planning and outlining

Some successful mystery writers are able to start writing a story with no more than an interesting character, a dramatic first scene, a snatch of witty dialogue, a compelling premise, or even just an opening line. They proceed on the faith that what they write will give them impetus to write more, and that the more they write, the more quickly the momentum will build.

It's a process of discovery for them. Their characters say and do surprising things and come to life as they emerge on the page, urging the writer forward.

Those who feel they don't need to know where their stories are going when they begin, who rely on their intuitive judgment, unquestionably have powerful instincts. As the words they have written push them along, schemes and concepts that reside in the fuzzy area between conscious and subconscious thought pull them forward. They develop and refine plans as they write. They need to get their story underway before they can fully imagine it. As they write, their minds begin to buzz with ideas, options, fragments, and images.

Other writers take the opposite approach. They will not write a single line until they have meticulously planned and outlined every scene in the story. They know exactly how the story will begin, how it will build to its climax, how it will be resolved, and how it will end. They know the life histories of all their characters and everything they will do and say. In effect, they finish all the creative work before they sit down to write the first page.

Planning and creativity

For beginning writers of mystery fiction, the most sensible approach emphasizes thorough planning and structuring while welcoming creativity and spontaneity. Think through and carefully organize the shape and development of your story, but always remain open to new ideas as you proceed. If you prefer to work from a long detailed outline, be willing to shift directions and alter it once your story is underway. Nothing fires the imagination like unleashing characters on the page. You should always listen to your imagination.

You can begin writing once you have asked all the "what if" questions, so you know how and why the crime was committed; you have thought hard and long about the dynamics between villain and victim; you know who your key characters are and how each one will either help your hero or complicate his quest—or, in some cases, do both.

At this point, your writing plan is a sequence of several key scenes that proceed according to cause-and-effect logic. These are the confrontations and major turning points that change your story's direction and are essential to its progress.

You know where you're going. You have a destination in the form of a climactic scene where the pieces of the puzzle will come together.

Don't begin writing until you have fully imagined these elements—sequence, the key scenes, and the climax. Write them down, expand them, give them detail. Before you try to write the first line of your story, construct a narrative outline. There may be plenty of gaps—unimagined scenes and bridges that you know must occur between the key plot points, characters you have not thought much about, subplots that you trust will grow organically from your story's central spine.

Outline and plan until you're sick of it. You'll know you're ready to start writing when you cannot bear the thought of planning and outlining for another minute.

By then your first scene is vivid in your mind, and you're eager to get it down on paper. You are confident that you will find the route to your story's first plot point, and from there you'll find your way to the second, and so on to the climax.

No matter how fully you've imagined your scenes or how excited you are about executing them, don't write scenes out of sequence. Let your key plot points work as writing goals for you. Let them pull you forward. They'll motivate you and make you eager to keep writing.

Know where you're going, and have at least a general idea of how to get there. But remain open-minded. Listen to your characters and follow the new ideas that emerge as your story unfolds. Be prepared to follow the new directions that did not occur to you in your original plan.

As you gain experience, you'll develop your own ways of combining planning with spontaneity. You may, for example, write your climactic scene first. Or you may write several key scenes, then fill in the spaces between them with the bridges and other scenes that link them. The more you write, the more likely you will be to develop an approach that combines careful planning with spontaneity. Learning how to take maximum advantage of thoughtful planning without stifling your own creativity comes from practice and experience.

Tempo, rhythm, and pace

Like a complex symphony, effective mystery fiction should unfold in ever-changing rhythms and tempos. It should alternate movements in allegro, andante, presto, and adagio. The tense dialogue scene needs a contemplative bridge before the car chase. The intrusion of the burglar is more dramatic when it interrupts a quiet love scene.

The sequence in which scenes occur must take into account pace and tempo as well as the demands of the storyline. The tense scenes in which Robert Parker's Spenser tracks down and confronts dangerous killers, for example, are broken up by quiet times in the kitchen and tender moments with Susan Silverman. Between interviewing suspects and witnesses, Sue Grafton's Kinsey Millhone goes jogging or visits Rosie's, her neighborhood bar. John D. MacDonald's Travis McGee takes a break from his confrontations with evil men to have a drink with Meyer, his philosophical friend. Many writers use humor to provide relief from suspense.

These changes of pace allow readers to pause, take a deep breath, process what has happened so far, and build up their anticipation for the next conflict. Your story is an experience for your readers. It shouldn't put them to sleep—but it shouldn't exhaust them, either.

Cliffhangers and other momentum builders

Thomas Harris ends a chapter in the middle of *The Silence of the Lambs* in the intimate point of view of Catherine Martin, who is imprisoned in a deep pit in a dark cellar:

> Except for shock and disorientation, it would not have been so long in coming to her. As it was, the skin emollient did it. Skin. She knew who had her then. The knowledge fell on her like every scalding awful thing on earth and she was screaming, screaming, under the futon, up and climbing, clawing at the wall, screaming until she was coughing something warm and salty in her mouth, hands to her face, drying sticky on the backs of her hands as she lay rigid on the futon, arching off the floor from head to heels, her hands clenched in her hair.

The next chapter begins:

> Clarice Starling's quarter bonged down through the telephone in the shabby orderlies' lounge. She dialed the van.

Catherine Martin is left there, trapped and screaming, for the reader to worry about while the story shifts to Clarice Starling's search. This is a classic cliffhanger.

In multiple point-of-view stories, scenes often end with the hero figuratively (and sometimes literally) hanging from a cliff by his fingertips. Will he manage to crawl to safety before the bad guy finds him and stomps on his hands? Will the heroine get there in time to rescue him before he loses his tenuous grip?

Sorry. He's left hanging there, and the story shifts to

the abandoned warehouse, where the heroine finds herself tied to a chair with a time bomb ticking under her. She struggles to untie the knots. The clock ticks away the seconds. . . .

The scene shifts again, this time to the villain, speeding across the desert in his pickup truck, pursued by his vengeful former partner. His tire blows out, he skids, his truck careens off the road. . . .

And so on. Every scene ends before it's resolved. Provided readers have come to care about what happens to the characters, cliffhangers keep them turning the pages.

Cliffhangers don't work the same way in the single point-of-view mystery. Readers walk only in the shoes of the heroine, who cannot proceed to search for her partner until she escapes from the warehouse. The hero cannot confront the villain until he pulls himself to safety from that cliff.

Some mystery writers, understanding that readers tend to stop reading at the end of chapter, keep them turning the pages by ending their chapters at a tense moment *in the middle of a scene*. Readers cannot put down a book when a character they care about has only ten seconds in extricate himself from that chair and race out of the warehouse before the bomb goes off. They must see how—or if—he does it. And so they keep reading.

The cliffhanger can be overused. If every chapter ends in the middle of the dialogue, or with the unexpected intrusion of a mysterious stranger, or with the ringing of the telephone, or with a gunshot, readers will begin to feel manipulated. They don't keep turning the pages just to see who says what next, or whether the mysterious stranger is friend or foe, or who's calling in the middle of the night, or whether the bullet hits anybody.

They keep reading because they care about the characters, are puzzled by the mystery, and have an emotional investment in the hero's quest.

If each scene does its job, it moves through the stages of goal, conflict, resolution, and new obstacle. It advances the story and creates a new problem for the hero, which builds genuine momentum and suspense and impels readers to move on to the next scene, and so on to the end of the story.

When it's done well, readers will say, "I couldn't put the book down." But if they decide to mark their place at the end of the chapter and turn out the light, that's O.K.—as long as they look forward to picking up your book again.

Cliffhanger chapter endings build short-term momentum. They work best in long complicated scenes—especially near the story's climax. Toward the end of *A Trouble of Fools*, for example, Linda Barnes ends a chapter this way:

Damn. There was the matter of the bartender. If it was the same bartender, old Billy what's-his-face, and if he remembered me, recalled my questions, my license, my card, I'd be sunk.

Maybe I'd have gone in anyway. Maybe I'd have taken some Pulitzer Prize photos, maybe I'd have gotten zip. I'll never know.

Flashing blue lights appeared out of nowhere, racing up behind me.

Shit. I smacked my horn in pure frustration, pulled over. The cops. Always there when you need them.

Readers are unlikely to stop reading here. But cliffhangers do not create a page-turning frenzy in readers if the story's other elements aren't working. And if those elements are used effectively, you don't need many cliff-hangers to keep your reader's attention.

Climax

The climax of a mystery story is the scene in which the key puzzle piece is found, enabling the hero or heroine to identify, confront, and subdue the villain. The final obstacle has been hurdled. The villain is revealed and justice is done.

Effective climactic scenes combine surprise, suspense, and satisfaction. Everything that has come before has led to this moment. Here, finally, the puzzle pieces all come together. The climax cannot be a let-down.

If readers have already solved the mystery, there is no surprise. It's an anticlimax, the sign of a failed story.

A suspenseful climax keeps readers in doubt until its resolution. Does the hero know what he's doing? Has he solved the puzzle correctly? Will the villain escape? Will the hero survive?

A satisfying climax brings together the thematic threads of the story. The puzzle pieces are assembled, the villain is identified and brought to justice, and the hero or heroine triumphs. When the story's moral questions are complex and contradictory, its resolution may be correspondingly ambiguous and ironic. But in mystery fiction, justice is served.

Climactic resolutions to avoid

Your heroine has solved the mystery. She's verified her suspicions, tracked down the villain to his hiding place, and now she confronts him. The problem, of course, is that this villain has killed one or more people as the story has progressed. He has proven to be a worthy adversary for your sleuth—elusive, clever, powerful, skilled, and determined to get away with his crimes.

Meanwhile, you have portrayed your heroine as smart and stubborn and highly motivated to solve the puzzle, but otherwise an average person, someone your readers can easily identify with.

Now she faces this worthy villain. How will she triumph? *Avoid* these solutions:

1. *Deux ex machina.* Greek plays sometimes ended with a character playing Zeus or Apollo or Hera being lowered by ropes and pulleys onto the stage. The god character then overpowered the villain, saved the heroine, and solved all of the other problems that had been created in the play. Greek audiences accepted the intervention of a god in their plays because they believed that the gods actively controlled the events in their own lives.

Few modern readers believe in meddling gods. They will not accept an ending in which coincidence or luck resolves what appears to be an impossible predicament. In western movies, the cavalry arrives just as twelve evil men are about to cut the throats of a helpless pioneer family. In detective stories, the police break down the door just as the villain is about to pull the trigger on the handgun he holds to your heroine's head.

If the arrival of the police or the cavalry or the night watchman or the heroine's loyal German shepherd has been planned, or if the savior's appearance makes sense because you've prepared your reader for it in advance, then it will not appear to be coincidence. If it flows logically from the story, in other words, it can work.

Here are some other examples of unsatisfactory endings that are tantamount to divine intervention: Your heroine, who has no particular experience with guns, kills the villain with a lucky shot; the villain, normally athletic and sure-footed, trips and falls and cracks his head on the corner of a table; an unexpected thunderstorm knocks out the electricity just as the villain reaches for your heroine's throat; the villain's car, in which he's carrying the bound-and-gagged heroine, runs out of gas in front of a police station.

Endings such as these are easy to write but hard for readers to swallow.

2. *The suddenly invincible hero or heroine.* You have created a desperate and resourceful villain. He has outwitted and overpowered and murdered several strong and capable people already. Now your heroine, using, for example, her skills at computer programming, has identified him. When she tells him what she knows, he says he must kill her to protect his secret. Your heroine then subdues him with karate kicks. Unless her karate expertise has been clearly established earlier in the story, this resolution will seem as contrived as the arrival of the cavalry.

3. *The suddenly fallible villain.* The police and the FBI have failed to bring your villain to justice. Everyone who has confronted him has been killed. Now, at the climactic moment, your heroine faces him—and he does something stupid or clumsy that allows her, unlike all those who have previously tried and failed, to subdue him.

This sort of unmotivated change in the villain is as unconvincing as the sudden invincibility of the heroine.

4. *The conversion of the villain.* Your heroine confronts the man who has murdered several people in cold blood. She condemns his evil ways. He nods and says, "You're absolutely right. I'm ready to give myself up. Take me in."

Unless you have portrayed your villain as a morally complex man, perhaps highly religious and tortured by his deeds, his sudden conversion will strike your reader as lucky and coincidental—another variation on the intervention of the gods.

Writing effective and believable climactic scenes requires all of your creativity. There is no formula. Your story's resolution must follow logically from the strengths and abilities and personalities of the characters and from the events that have come before. And yet it must not seem preordained. The climax must bring all of your story's tension and conflict to a peak. It's the moment when the forces of good and evil confront each other. Make it believable, make it logical—and make it a surprise.

Denouement

In the denouement that follows the climactic scene, the mystery's solution is explained and order is restored. Here the stray puzzle pieces are gathered and sorted and the tangled threads are unraveled. All of the confusing and seemingly random events that have occurred, and all of the characters who have appeared in the story, are rearranged into a logical pattern. Subplots and secondary conflicts such as romantic relationships are resolved. The order destroyed by the murder at the story's outset is now reestablished.

In some cases the climax can incorporate the story's denouement. The hero or heroine assembles the clues in a logical way. She tracks down the villain, confronts him, subdues him, and levels her accusation. The villain admits his guilt and confirms the heroine's suspicions. Remaining questions of motive and means and the roles of other characters are answered in the climactic scene.

When the climax leaves significant questions unanswered, however, an additional scene, the denouement, is necessary. Readers are disappointed if the story ends with plot threads left dangling.

Beware of long rambling confessions. In real life, villains don't typically bare their souls to the good guys who best them. Fictional villains shouldn't, either. Avoid denouements in which the point-of-view character—either in question-and-answer dialogue with another character or in narration directed at the reader—explains how he or she figured it all out. The climax should resolve as much of the story as possible, and the denouement should be completed in two or three short scenes.

Remember: The story is the sleuth's quest of detection. When he or she solves the puzzle, the story is effectively over.

Prologues and epilogues

A prologue is usually a short, focused, single scene showing an event that occurred before the time in which the story itself unfolds. Similarly, an epilogue concerns events that occur after the story's climax and denouement.

A prologue and an epilogue can give symmetry to a mystery, but they can also make it appear that the writer is striving to be "literary." If you are tempted to add a prologue and/or an epilogue as an afterthought, scrutinize your reasons. Most well-told stories don't need either.

A story about an escaped convict who murders the jurors who sent him to prison ten years earlier, for example, might benefit from a prologue in which the convict's original crime is dramatized. If the storyline involves the murder (or was it suicide?) of a disabled Vietnam veteran, try a prologue that recounts the circumstances under which the vet was wounded.

In Rick Boyer's *Pirate Trade*, his narrator, Doc Adams, explains in a prologue called "Lightship Purse" the origin of the baskets crafted by Nantucket natives and the significance of the ivory medallions on their lids. The reader needs this information to understand the story that follows.

James Lee Burke opens *Black Cherry Blues* with a dream sequence that establishes the foreboding mood of the novel and introduces the reader to the tortured mind of Dave Robicheaux, the first-person narrator.

If your prologue sets a mood, reveals a character trait, gives important information, or introduces a theme echoed in the story itself, it is likely to work for you. If it does none of these things, delete it.

Epilogues typically explain what happens to characters after the story has ended. Minette Walters ends *The Sculptress* with this epilogue:

> At 5:30 on a dark and frosty winter morning the Sculptress walked free from the gates of her prison, two hours earlier than the time announced to the press. She had sought and obtained permission to slip back into society well away from the glare of publicity that had surrounded the release of other celebrated cases of wrongful imprisonment. Roz and Sister Bridget, alerted by telephone, stood outside in the lamplight, stamping their feet and blowing on their hands. They smiled in welcome as the Judas door opened.
>
> Only Hal, sheltering ten yards away in the warmth of the car, saw the look of gloating triumph that swept briefly over Olive's face as she put her arms around the two women and lifted them bodily into the air. He recalled some words that he'd had stencilled on his desk when he was still a policeman. *'Truth lies within a little and certain compass, but error is immense.'*
>
> For no apparent reason, he shivered.

This epilogue, which takes place a significant time after the story itself has ended, is necessary to give the reader a sense of completion. In this case, what happens to Olive Martin after the story itself ends contains a hint of irony and foreboding. The epilogue in *The Sculptress* is dramatically satisfying. It leaves something for the reader to speculate about: Is Olive Martin *really* innocent?

≈ 9 ≈

Building Conflict to Make Scenes Work

ALL FORMS OF FICTION—films, stage plays, novels, short stories—unfold in an ordered sequence of events or scenes, the purpose of which is to move the story forward. In mystery fiction, each scene is a turn along the maze of the sleuth's journey of detection. If you neglect to account for even one of those turns, your reader will become immediately—and hopelessly—lost.

Every scene should have a function. Test its validity by asking yourself: "If I omitted this scene completely, would the story still make sense to my readers? Would my hero still get to the same place at the end?"

If your answer is "yes," you should omit the scene.

While moving the story forward through time and space, scenes perform other functions as well. They introduce new characters. They expand and complicate the personalities and motivations of old characters. They establish setting and mood. They develop subplots, clues, red herrings, and false trails. They amuse, sadden, excite, confuse, clarify, educate.

Scenes dramatize events that are *motivated*. Accident, coincidence, and luck, while common enough in real life, do not move invented stories believably. Readers want to know *why* events occur. They demand cause-and-effect logic. The law of stimulus-response operates in well-motivated novels and short stories. For everything that happens there must be a reason. Readers may not immediately know what that reason is; in fact, *not* knowing impels them to continue reading. They trust that explanations will eventually emerge, and they read on, seeking clues that will help them understand the stimuli that produced the responses they witnessed. If those explanations never appear, or if the only explanation is luck or coincidence, readers feel cheated.

Scenes should create the illusion of taking place in *real time*. Action is played out step by step. Dialogue scenes unfold word by word, fight scenes blow by blow, love scenes caress by caress. No significant piece of action is omitted in a scene. As readers witness these events, the illusion becomes their reality. They are there.

You can, and sometimes should, summarize actions: "O'Donnell, the bad cop, questioned the woman for an hour. Then Napoli took over. He played the good cop. He got nothing out of her, either." Or, "They scratched and punched and pulled each other's hair, and then the two women fell to the floor exhausted." Or, "We kissed and stroked each other long into the night."

But while summaries do important storytelling work, they do not create the illusion of observed events for readers. Summaries are not scenes.

Every character in mystery fiction, as we have seen, wants something important that he doesn't have, cannot get without struggle, and is willing to take risks to gain. The sleuth, the truth-seeker, struggles to solve the mystery, while the villain does everything he can to escape detection. Every other character has a direct or indirect stake in the story's outcome. Tension and suspense come from characters whose goals conflict with each other.

A scene can be defined as a closely connected sequence of actions in which one or more characters working toward an important goal encounter obstacles, struggle against those obstacles, achieve some kind of resolution, and end up with new problems. The new problems lead to new efforts to achieve their goals, which are dramatized in subsequent scenes, and so on to the climax.

Every scene, therefore, contains GOAL, OBSTACLE, CONFLICT, RESOLUTION, and NEW OBSTACLE. Eliminate any one of these elements and your scene falls flat.

Let's analyze a typical scene in mystery fiction, this one from *The Sculptress* by Minette Walters. Roz, a writer and the story's protagonist, has agreed to write a book about Olive Martin, a convicted murderess. Roz visits Olive in prison and then does some background research on the unspeakably violent murder of the woman's mother and her sister. Roz is repelled. She cannot bear the thought of spending more time with Olive and writing about it. She decides to tell Iris, her agent, that the deal is off:

> She seized the telephone and dialled Iris's number. "Have I signed anything on the Olive Martin book? Why? Because I damn well can't write it, that's why. The woman scares the bloody shit out of me and I am not visiting her again."
>
> "I thought you liked her." Iris spoke calmly through a mouthful of supper.
>
> Roz ignored this comment. "I've got her statement here and the pathologist's report, or his conclusions at least. I should have read them first. I'm not doing it. I will not glorify what she did by writing a book about it. My God, Iris, they were alive when she cut their heads off. Her poor wretched mother tried to ward off the axe. It's making me sick just thinking about it."

"OK."

"OK what?"

"Don't write it."

Roz's eyes narrowed suspiciously. "I thought you'd argue at least."

"Why? One thing I've learnt in this business is that you can't force people to write. Correction. You can if you're persistent and manipulative enough, but the result is always below par." Roz heard her take a drink. 'In any case, Jenny Atherton sent me the first ten chapters of her new book this morning. It's all good stuff on the inherent dangers of a poor self-image, with obesity as number one confidence crippler. She's unearthed a positive goldmine of film and television personalities who've all sunk to untold depths since gaining weight and being forced off camera. It's disgustingly tasteless, of course, like all Jenny's books, but it'll sell. I think you should send all your gen—sorry about the pun—to her. Olive would make a rather dramatic conclusion, don't you think, particularly if we can get a photograph of her in her cell.'

"No chance."

"No chance of getting a photograph? Shame."

"No chance of my sending anything to Jenny Atherton. Honestly, Iris,' she stormed, losing her temper, 'you really are beneath contempt. You should be working for the gutter press. You believe in exploiting anyone just as long as they bring in the cash. Jenny Atherton is the last person I'd allow near Olive."

"Can't see why," said Iris, now chewing heartily on something. 'I mean if you don't want to write about her and you're refusing ever to visit her again because she makes you sick, why cavil at somebody else having a bash?"

"It's the principle."

"Can't see it, old thing. Sounds more like dog in the manger to me. Listen, I can't dally. We've got people in. At least let me tell Jenny that Olive's up for grabs. She can start from scratch. It's not as though you've got very far, is it?"

"I've changed my mind," Roz snapped. "I will do it. Good-
bye." She slammed the receiver down.

This scene moves the story. Roz's reluctance to become involved with Olive Martin is crucial to the story's
development. On the other hand, unless she does continue to visit Olive, there is no story. Roz begins with
the goal of abandoning the story. Iris, knowing how Roz
will respond, cleverly creates the obstacle of readily
agreeing and suggests that Jenny Atherton, Roz's rival,
can take over the project. Now Roz faces a conflict: If
she gives up the project, Jenny will get it; if she continues her interviews with Olive Martin, she will be forced
to deal with a person who repels her. Roz resolves the
conflict by staying on the project, which creates a new
obstacle for her: Now she must continue her research
into a story that she finds highly offensive.

The scene does other work besides committing the
reluctant Roz to write about Olive Martin. It character-
izes Roz as uncertain in her convictions, sensitive and
emotional, and easily manipulated—all traits that become important later in the story. The scene emphasizes
Roz's powerful response to Olive Martin. And it shows
that Iris knows how to get her way with Roz.

The law of stimulus-response motivates the characters
in this scene. Roz calls Iris to beg off the project. Iris
responds by readily agreeing—which, as Iris expects,
causes Roz to respond by changing her mind.

The scene gives the illusion of taking place in real
time. It contains no summary of events or condensation
of time. The conversation between Roz and Iris is played
out in its entirety. The attributions in the dialogue and
the descriptions of the characters' actions appear to con-
sume all of the pauses in the conversation. Thus readers

sense that it takes them as long to read the scene as it would take actually to witness it.

Building bridges

A work of fiction is not constructed entirely of scenes. Some events should be summarized, as we have seen. The passage of time between events needs to be suggested, and the consequences of a scene sometimes need to be pondered.

The bridges or transitions between scenes take various forms:

1. *Summary of intervening events.* What happens between the scenes may be uninteresting, unimportant, or unproductive. It does not contain the conflict elements that would make it a scene, but it still needs to be accounted for. In *Cruel and Unusual* Patricia Cornwell simply writes: "I tried Marino and he wasn't home or at headquarters." Nothing more is needed.

2. *Indication of elapsed time.* Whether it's a few minutes, hours, or even months or years, you must keep your readers informed about the passage in time between scenes. For example, in *F Is for Fugitive*, Sue Grafton accounts for a hunk of time this way: "After supper, I snagged a jacket from my room and headed down the back stairs."

3. *Analysis of the ramifications of the preceding scene.* Pause before the next scene to interpret and consider the implications of the scene that has just ended. Periodically in mystery fiction readers need to stop, stretch, and take a deep breath. Things have been moving fast. There's a lot to ponder for both the sleuth and the reader. Before you move forward to the next scene, you should help your readers understand what's happened so far and how the last scene affects the story. Here's how Dick Francis does this in *Straight:*

Perhaps I had been imagining things: but I knew I hadn't. One could often hear more nuances in someone's voice on the telephone than one could face to face. When people were relaxed, the lower vibration of their voices came over the wires undisturbed; under stress, the lower vibrations disappeared because the vocal cords involuntarily tightened. After Loder had discovered I would be inheriting Dozen Roses, there had been no lower vibrations at all.

4. *Consideration of future actions.* What should the sleuth do next? How can he use what he's learned in the preceding scene? What are his alternatives? Unless you share your sleuth's thinking with your readers, they will feel unprepared for the next scene. In *Skinwalkers,* Tony Hillerman uses this bridge:

> Leaphorn put the memo aside. When the more normal working day began, he'd call Largo and see if he had anything to add. But now he wanted to think about his three homicides.

Bridges can be as brief as a phrase or sentence, or they can go on for several paragraphs. Their purpose is to move the protagonist smoothly from one scene to the next. Bridges are not always necessary or desirable, and sometimes you can omit them entirely by starting a new chapter or inserting a line break, then beginning the next scene directly. In many cases you can trust your readers to fill in the gap between the two sequential scenes without explanation. The next scene logically comes next, and readers can follow along without being told what has happened or how much time has elapsed between them.

The bridges that connect scenes are by their nature passive and introspective. They are summaries that come directly to the reader from the story's narrative point of view. They do not take place in real time, and they lack all of the other elements of scenes.

All fiction needs bridges. But keep them to a minimum, keep them brief, and keep them focused. When writing bridges, it's tempting to theorize, philosophize, speculate, recapitulate, rhapsodize, and expound. When you do too much of this, your story's momentum grinds to a halt. Mystery readers don't pick up your book to learn your views on life and love and death. They care about your story's characters and their problems.

≈ 10 ≈

Dialogue: The Lifeblood of Mystery Fiction

B ECAUSE YOUR SLEUTH can't be everywhere at once, she cannot witness all of your story's crucial events. If she actually saw the crime as it was committed, of course, then there would be no mystery. For the same reason, she cannot overhear conversations in which the culprit reveals his motives, divulges his plans, or confesses his guilt.

That's why dialogue between the protagonist and other key characters is so important in mystery fiction. Although the hero or heroine must be active and participate in and witness many events firsthand, it's largely through conversations with others that the sleuth (and the reader) gathers clues. Thus the primary method for information-gathering in mystery fiction is the interrogation, although it's rarely a simple matter of asking questions and receiving answers. The sleuth understands that the various people she encounters have their own agendas. Some characters refuse to cooperate. Some become belligerent. Some lie or withhold information. Others distort the truth for their own private, and sometimes subconscious, reasons. These lies and distortions can create new directions for investigation, some of which may prove productive while others turn out to be false trails and dead-ends.

Sometimes characters divulge key information without intending to—information that becomes significant only later, after other clues have been collected.

More than other forms of fiction, the mystery calls upon dialogue to perform multiple tasks, such as delineate character, create conflict, build tension, establish mood, present clues, suggest false trails, and give momentum to the story. An effective dialogue scene can accomplish all of these jobs in a few seemingly simple and straightforward exchanges. Because of the special importance of dialogue in mystery fiction, the writer simply must master the art of recreating conversations that are clear, entertaining, and realistic while performing the vital clue-gathering function.

Writing dialogue that sounds real

The conversations that we engage in and overhear in real life tend to be repetitious, semi-articulate, and boring. Transcripts of such conversations, while authentic, would make tedious reading, and the writer who tries to recreate it literally risks writing muddy and hard-to-read dialogue.

In real life, for example, this is how a woman might try to explain to her male friend that she doesn't want him to spend the night with her:

> "I don't—that is, well, I'm sorry, but . . ."
> "I, um, I mean, you sure? That I can't stay?"
> "Well, not, you know, not tonight, I think. Just, not tonight."
> "Yeah, well, okay, I guess."
> "You do—um, do you understand?"

"Well, I guess not really, I don't."
"It's, like, well, sort of confusing."
"Can you, I mean, why don't you try to, ah, explain it to me, huh?"
"Sure, okay. See, I guess I—well, really, to tell you the truth, I just sort of want to, um, be alone."

This exchange is "realistic," but it's not readable. Effectively written dialogue creates sparse and clear speech that wastes no words and yet sounds authentic. But simply eliminating the redundant and inarticulate parts is not enough; it produces flat, lifeless dialogue.
For example:

"Not tonight."
"Okay."
"Do you understand?"
"No."
"It's complicated."
"Try me."
"Okay. I want to be alone."
"You mean, you want to be apart from me."
"Yes."

It's impossible to read this exchange without losing track of which character is which, of course, but otherwise this dialogue is sharper and easier to read. The message comes across clearly, cleanly, and concisely. But it lacks impact. It fails to suggest the powerful mixture of emotions that the characters must be feeling—emotions that were more strongly conveyed in the first version.
One way to correct this is to write dialogue in which the characters talk about their feelings. They can reassure each other of their love and tell each other of the pain and conflict they are feeling. Unless handled with

extreme restraint, however, direct expressions of emotion tend to sound maudlin and overblown and inconsistent with the characters' personalities. They do not ring true.

For example:

> "I'm sorry. It hurts me so much to have to say this to you. I'm very fond of you. I love you. Don't ever forget that. It's been wonderful, what we've had. I'm just very confused right now. Please understand."
>
> "Don't worry about it. I'll be fine. It hurts. A lot. But I'll manage somehow."

Here the writer has taken the easy way out by having the characters say exactly what they are feeling and thinking. There is no drama in a conversational exchange that tells rather than shows.

Another form of telling rather than showing in dialogue substitutes highly expressive verbs and descriptive adverbs for the characters' own expressions of emotion:

> "I'm sorry," she murmured sadly.
>
> "Don't worry about it," he growled through clenched teeth.
>
> "Tonight I need to be alone," she whispered tearfully. "Just tonight," she sobbed. "Okay?" she asked hopefully.

The characters' emotions in this version are absolutely clear. The expressive verbs ("murmured," "growled," "whispered") and the descriptive adverbs ("sadly," "tearfully," "hopefully") leave no doubt in the reader's mind.

The problem here is that the writer has intruded on the scene to explain what is happening in the characters' minds. The reader is yanked out of the point-of-view character's shoes. The author has intervened to remind readers in no uncertain terms that there is indeed a diligent writer at work, controlling their reactions by telling them what's going on and interpreting it for them—and, in the process, depriving them of the opportunity to gather clues and use their imaginations. When that happens, readers don't identify or empathize with the characters; they remain passive observers. The intrusive writer has destroyed the potential emotional impact of the scene by overexplaining it.

Truly effective dialogue, like all writing, must show without telling. It works, like an effective film scene, through pictures and dialogue alone. The writer must remain invisible. What is *not* stated shows as much about the characters as what they say and do.

In addition to the spoken words themselves, dialogue writers have two other tools. The first, attribution, should be used sparingly. Its primary purpose is simply to prevent the reader from getting the speakers confused. Not every statement requires attribution. The most useful attribution is "said" because, in dialogue scenes, an occasional "he said"—*without* an explanatory adverb—works as an invisible signpost. It registers, but does not intrude on the reader's involvement in the scene.

Attributions should be inserted into dialogue where they are least intrusive and noticeable—normally in the *first natural pause* in the spoken sentence. In this way, the attribution contributes to the rhythm of the dialogue without calling attention to itself.

Note how the placement of the attributions is less noticeable and enhances the rhythm better in the second of the following two pieces of dialogue:

"Tonight I need to be alone. Just tonight. Okay?" she said.

I said, "You got it."

Or:

"Tonight," she said, "I need to be alone. Just tonight. Okay?'

"You got it," I said.

The second tool in writing good dialogue is what stage actors call "business," the combination of gesture and body language that are incidental to the main action—the conversation—but that suggest feelings and contribute visually to the audience's understanding of the scene. Actors know that the smallest gesture, if well-timed and carefully chosen, can communicate a great deal, whereas elaborate and overblown gestures and actions are distracting and intrusive. Writers, like actors, should avoid overacting.

In dialogue, a piece of business can be used instead of attribution, thereby doing double duty. In the following example, there is no need for the attribution "she said," because the character's actions make it perfectly clear who's speaking:

She put her arms around my neck and her cheek on my shoulder. "It's complicated."

The judicious use of attribution and business frees the writer from having to intrude on the scene to tell the reader, "There was a long moment of silence," or, "He hesitated briefly before he continued."

Here's how Carl Hiaasen combines sparse dialogue,

attribution, and business in what is essentially an interrogation scene in his novel *Native Tongue:*

> Joe Winder wanted to talk about what happened in Talla-
> hassee. "I read all the stories," he said. "I went back and
> looked up the microfiche."
> "Then you know all there is to know." Skink was on his
> haunches, poking the embers with a stick. Winder refused
> to look at what was frying in the pan.
> He said, "All this time and they never found you."
> "They quit searching," Skink said. A hot ash caught in a
> wisp of his beard. He snuffed it with two fingers. "I don't
> normally eat soft-shell turtle," he allowed.
> "Me neither," said Joe Winder.

Hiaasen manages to convey a great deal about the two
characters in this simple dialogue scene without describing them. We sense the tension between Winder, who
seeks information, and Skink, who is reluctant to give it
to him. The scene is highly visual, yet the reader never
loses track of the conversation.

In the following fragment of a straightforward interrogation scene from *A Is for Alibi*, Sue Grafton mingles
business with dialogue to create a memorable character:

> "Are you Sharon Napier?" I asked.
> She looked up. Her eyes were rimmed with dark lashes,
> the green taking on an almost turquoise hue in the fluores-
> cent light overhead.
> "I don't think we've met," she said.
> "I'm Kinsey Millhone," I said. "May I sit down?"
> She shrugged by way of consent. She took a compact out
> of her pocket and checked her eye makeup, removing a
> slight smudge of shadow from her upper lid. Her lashes
> were clearly false, but the effect was flashy, giving her eyes
> an exotic slant. She applied fresh lip gloss, using her little

finger, which she dipped into a tiny pot of pink. "What can I do for you?" she asked, glancing up briefly from her compact mirror.

"I'm looking into the death of Laurence Fife."

Some dialogue pitfalls

1. *Windbags.* Avoid rambling monologues, long speeches, and one-sided lectures. Try to keep dialogue exchanges terse and to the point. Never allow the reader to lose track of the setting or of the fact that there are at least two participants in the dialogue scene. If your scene requires one character to talk at length while the other remains essentially passive, find ways to break up the speech. Your second character might interrupt and tell the speaker to get to the point. A waitress might appear to take their dinner order. Or the speaker himself might pause to relight his pipe, sip his drink, or scratch his head.

Eyeball your dialogue scenes. If a page of dialogue is solid print from margin to margin, it's too dense. Break it up. A page of readable dialogue should have a lot of white space and ragged margins.

2. *Crowded scenes.* As a practical matter, dialogue scenes with more than two participants are cumbersome for the writer and confusing for the reader. For one thing, when three or more characters are talking, every statement requires attribution or business to clarify who's speaking. More important, the dynamics among several speakers are multiplied geometrically. Two characters constitute a single well-focused relationship. With three characters, there are three relationships for you and your readers to keep track of. When each of four characters interacts with the other three, there are six separate relationships to follow, and with five characters there are ten, and so on.

Three-character dialogue scenes can be managed if one of the characters—usually your point-of-view protagonist—plays the role of observer or mediator, thus keeping the focus on the dynamic between the other two participants. In general, avoid dialogue scenes involving more than three characters.

3. *Exposition through dialogue.* In real life, people do not tell each other what they both already know. Your fictional characters shouldn't do it, either. It's not an effective way to feed information to the reader.

For example:

> "You're a big guy," he said. "You must be at least six-two and, what, two-forty? I'm just a shrimp. I'm only five-seven and I weigh one-fifty soaking wet. And you've got all those scars on your face and those mean shifty eyes. . . ."

Or:

> "We've been through a lot together, Joe. You and I were in the Marines together. We trained at Parris Island before they shipped us to Chu Lai in '68. We shared a hooch. We saved each other's butt a dozen times. We took our R and R in Australia. And we fell in love with the same woman. That Aussie, Wanda, from Sidney. The tall blonde who was addicted to crossword puzzles and cocaine. She had that old boyfriend, remember? Pete. Yeah, that was his name. Pete Thompson, the air-conditioner repairman, who . . ."

Scenes such as these do not ring true. In fact, it sounds like poorly disguised exposition—the writer's crude attempt to convert straight narrative into dialogue.

4. *Bores.* In real life, most of the conversations we overhear—or engage in ourselves—are aimless and

mundane. The writer's challenge is to create dialogue that seems true-to-life but is never boring. Strive for wit, irony, and cleverness. Scintillating dialogue emerges naturally from fascinating characters—and vice versa. Give each of your characters a distinctive speaking voice and style. Remember: Boring dialogue makes boring fiction.

5. *Dialogue for its own sake.* Trying to write clever or amusing dialogue for its own sake, on the other hand, is self-indulgent. Unless your dialogue *advances the story*, readers will quickly decide that those witty characters are talking to hear themselves talk and to amuse each other, and that the writer is just showing off.

6. *Dialect.* Because it requires readers to "translate" it, dialogue heavy with dialect is distracting. It tends to distance readers from the characters and the movement of the plot. Moreover, faithful reproduction of dialect risks parody and can be interpreted as insulting and demeaning.

On the other hand, you can't ignore the fact that some characters speak in dialect and have distinctive verbal habits. The trick is to *suggest* dialect rather than replicate it. For example, let your teen-aged characters begin some (but not all) of their sentences with their favorite throwaway word, "Like." Your Down East lobsterman might mutter "Ayuh" occasionally (but not every time he speaks), and your Midwesterner can pronounce the nation's capital "Warshington." If your city-dwelling African-American character says "ax" when he means "ask" and "yo" when he means "yes," your readers will fill in the rest for themselves.

In the following exchange from *Black Cherry Blues*, notice how James Lee Burke underplays the dialect and speech patterns of the Cajun character Batist:

"Them people that make the movie, they put it in that box, huh, Dave?" he said.

"That's right."

"Then how it get up to the antenna and in the set?"

"It doesn't go up to —"

"And how come it don't go in nobody else's set?" he said.

"It don't go out the house," Alafair said.

"Not 'It don't.' Say 'It doesn't,'" I said.

"Why you telling her that? She talk English good as us," Batist said.

7. *Four-letter words.* In real life, some people use certain words and phrases habitually, some only under certain circumstances, and some not to all. For dialogue to be technically realistic, some characters may need to use four-letter words, depending on their personality, their background, and their role in your story.

Most contemporary best-selling mystery fiction includes characters who use this language. Four-letter words help delineate the characters who use them and, by contrast, characterize those who don't.

There are readers, however, who are so offended by certain words that they refuse to read books in which this language appears, no matter how realistically. Writers must choose between the rock of authenticity and the hard place of automatic elimination of sensitive or conservative readers from their fan clubs.

Fine-tuning your ear for dialogue

If editors and readers comment that your dialogue sounds stilted and false, the following exercises may help you to fine-tune it:

1. Read and analyze those writers whose dialogue sings. Ed McBain, Robert Parker, Sue Grafton, Lawrence Block, Sara Paretsky, George V. Higgins, James Lee Burke, and Elmore Leonard are among our contem-

porary masters. In fact, there are very few successful mystery authors who *don't* write effective dialogue.

2. Listen to films or television dramas with your eyes closed. Try to "hear" the emotions and unspoken agendas of the characters. Visualize their gestures and behavior from listening to their speech.

3. Read your own dialogue *aloud*. Even better, have somebody read it to you. Your ear will pick up the false notes that your eye may miss.

4. Eavesdrop on real-life conversations. Listen for the pauses, hesitations, repetitions, and verbal habits that real people use. Then sit down at your keyboard, close your eyes, and try to "hear" those conversations. First try to reproduce them verbatim. Then edit what you've written, adding attribution and business, until it flows smoothly and sounds authentic.

Sparkling, true-to-life dialogue is the foundation of mystery fiction. The trickiest plot twist, the most dynamic cast of characters, the most vivid setting, and the most hair-raising action will not ring true unless your characters talk like real people.

≈ 11 ≈

Getting It Right: Rewriting and Revising

W HEN I COMPLETED MY second mystery novel (the first one having been retired to the attic), I circulated a synopsis and three sample chapters and received my share of rejections. So when the editor asked to see the entire manuscript, I was, naturally, elated, and I shipped it to New York by return mail.

Several weeks later I received this letter: "We think you are a good writer. But you've made several typical beginner's blunders. The plot lacks originality. The story lacks suspense. We knew who the culprit was right away. We can't offer you a contract for your book in its present form, but if you'd be willing to rewrite it, we'd be interested in looking at it again."

Rewrite it? I thought. I had just spent more than a year writing, rewriting, and revising that book until it was, I believed, the very best I could make it.

And now they were telling me it still wasn't good enough.

I read and reread that letter. I had arrived, I realized, at a crisis in my writing career. If I *could* rewrite the book to that editor's satisfaction, I'd be on my way.

If I couldn't, I would probably never write a publishable novel.

It seemed that clear-cut to me.

It took me a year to untangle the original storyline and rework it, to reimagine the characters, to refine the book's narrative voice, to discard old scenes and to think up new ones. It was the most difficult job of writing I have ever undertaken.

But the new version of my book was accepted and, in due course, published. It even won an award. And since then, I've published twelve more mysteries featuring Brady Coyne, the first-person narrator of that first one.

Writing the original—flawed—version of that book had been hard.

Rewriting it was agonizing.

But getting it accepted, signing a contract, receiving a check in the mail, and eventually, holding a slick hardcover edition of *my* book in my hand—all of that was a great deal of fun.

The experience taught me what it meant to be a writer: You must be prepared to sit in front of a keyboard when it's the last thing you want to do, and do it regularly, day after day, for as long as it takes to string together thousands upon thousands of perfectly chosen and ordered words that will grab the reader and refuse to let go.

It's work. Writers are like everybody else. Much of the time they'd rather play than work.

On the other hand, if it were easy, everyone would write books. Most people don't, although a great many people say they would like to, and almost everyone is envious of those who do.

Thousands of unpublished manuscripts languish in desk drawers and attics and closets, and for every one of them there are thousands of first chapters and half-finished novels. Writing is like exercising: It begins with a burst of inspiration and good intentions, but it's sustained through all the pain and self-doubt and imperceptible progress and failure by hard-nosed commitment and steely discipline.

It's a hard job, and there's no avoiding that fact. If you want to write mystery fiction, be prepared for it.

But because it's hard, it's correspondingly satisfying.

Peter De Vries said it all: "I love being a writer. What I can't stand is the paperwork."

On writing well

A mystery story that fails to present intriguing characters, a fascinating world, and a suspenseful and complex puzzle, no matter how well it's written, will rarely be published.

The converse, however, is equally true, especially for the beginning writer: A clever storyline, *unless it's well written*, will not sell a book.

There are exceptions to both of these truths. Marvelous writing occasionally sells flawed stories, and fast-paced page-turners that are executed crudely sometimes get published.

You should derive encouragement from these exceptions. "I can write better than *this*," you should say. Or, "I can create a better story than *this* one."

But never think that agents, publishers and readers of mystery fiction don't care about craftsmanship. Nowadays few editors have the time or the inclination to fix your verbs, cut your scenes, or sharpen your images. You've got to be your own editor. Take pride in your writing. Examine every word and phrase. A well-written manuscript deprives agents and editors of one reason to reject it.

A detailed analysis of the elements of good writing is

beyond the scope of this book. But here, briefly, are some of the important principles of effective mystery writing:

1. Good writing *does not call attention to itself or the writer.* Flowery language, convoluted sentences, and ten-dollar words may cause the reader to think, "My goodness, this writer is awfully clever." But if the writing distracts the reader, it fails to do its job.

2. Good writing *tells the story.* It invites the reader to become immersed in the lives, problems, and goals of the characters. That's its job.

3. Good writing *engages the reader's feelings.* It evokes an emotional response. It makes readers *care* about the story's characters and what happens to them.

4. Good writing comes from *strong, active verbs.* Test the effectiveness of your prose by circling your verbs. How many times have you used "was" and "were" and other forms of "to be," or equally flat and flabby intransitive verbs such as "seemed" and "appeared"? Change them. Convert instances of the passive voice into the active form. In good writing, active verbs make things happen. Inactive verbs shift the burden to adjectives and adverbs, which are inherently passive.

5. Good writing *shows.* It does *not tell.* It emphasizes scenes where events occur. It minimizes exposition, explanation, description, and summary. Instead of telling us that a character is sad or angry or frightened, good writing *shows* us the character's behavior and allows us to draw our own conclusions. *Telling* relies on adjectives and adverbs; *showing* comes from active, vivid verbs.

6. Good writing is *concise and clear and efficient.* It wastes no words. It does its job quietly. As Elmore Leonard advises, "leave out the parts that people skip."

7. Good writing, in other words, is *invisible.* It appears so effortless that readers don't notice it. Good

writing is a sleight-of-hand trick. It gives the illusion of ease and simplicity.

Writers work hard to create that illusion. "Easy reading," said Nathaniel Hawthorne, "is damned hard writing."

After the first draft

Dorothy Parker once said, "I can't write five words but that I change seven."

"Nothing you write," said Lillian Hellman, "if you hope to be any good, will ever come as you first hoped."

Writing a novel or short story is like sculpting a statue. The first draft gives it shape and proportion. But it inevitably needs refining and polishing.

The first revision. Once you've written the first draft of any piece of fiction, put it aside. Work on something else and try not to think about it for several weeks. Then read it over with a fresh eye. Try to judge it the way a reader—or an editor—might. Look for the boring parts, the inconsistencies, the dangling plot threads, the pointless subplots. Try to think about all of the elements that make stories work for readers. You'll undoubtedly have to rewrite some scenes, delete others, and add new ones. Think about tempo and rhythm, plot development, character motivation.

Be alert to inconsistencies and errors of fact. Pay close attention to the details. Fiction readers bring to stories a "willing suspension of disbelief." They want to enter the world you have created, and they are prepared to accept the reality of that world and the characters who inhabit it. But a single error or inconsistency, no matter how small, can destroy that willingness to suspend their disbelief. Mystery readers know their guns and poisons and forensics. Mystery writers must know at least as much as their readers. Never confuse a revolver with an automatic or a shotgun with a rifle or gauge with caliber.

Here are four rules that will help you avoid losing readers because of small errors in detail:

1. When possible, write about what you know. Choose settings where you have lived, or at least visited. Give your characters—especially your protagonists—your own profession and hobbies. Use your life experiences as the basis for plots and character conflicts.

2. When you've got to do research, be thorough. Inevitably, you'll have to explore foreign worlds. Your story will require you to create characters such as medical specialists whose work you don't understand. You'll need to know precisely how a government bureaucracy, or a court, or a hospital deals with a situation that arises in your story.

Library research, of course, is essential. But take the next step. Solicit the help of professionals. If your story needs a scene with a forensic pathologist, interview a forensic pathologist. Ask her exactly how the situation in your story would be handled. After you write the scene, ask her to read it for you. Encourage her to identify every problem, no matter how minor. Most people enjoy contributing to the creation of a novel or short story and are flattered to be asked.

3. Don't try to impress your readers. Having completed all of this research, it's tempting to use it all. This typically produces long-winded and pointless passages where you show off all of the fascinating material you've worked so hard to master. Examine these sections carefully and be prepared to cut. Your story isn't a catch-all for everything you know and have learned. If it doesn't move your story forward, the passage doesn't belong.

Sometimes you'll find your story needs a major overhaul on its first revision. Sometimes it just needs fine-tuning. But it will always need something.

The second revision. After you're confident you've got the shape of the story right, and after you've double-checked it for technical accuracy, it's time to put a shine on your manuscript. Go back to the beginning and examine each word and punctuation mark, each sentence and paragraph. Hack away flabby adverbs and adjectives, look critically at every verb, listen to your dialogue. Try for absolute clarity in your prose and delete any self-indulgent flights of literary fancy, aiming to follow Samuel Johnson's advice: "Read over your compositions and, when you meet a passage which you think is particularly fine, strike it out."

Some writers find this polishing process tedious, but most enjoy it. At this stage, you've already done the hard part. You've invented a complicated story and all of its elements. You've assembled all of the elements into a novel-length manuscript. This tinkering and refining is your reward.

When you've finished this final polish, you should believe you have written a perfect story.

Mentors. But, of course, you can't completely trust your own judgment. So when you feel that you cannot possibly improve your manuscript, ask someone else to read it—someone whom you absolutely trust to tell you the truth, an experienced writer and reader who understands the kind of fiction you write, who has a sharp eye and ear, and who knows that you *want* the unvarnished truth. You must not ask for praise from your mentor. You want honest criticism.

Friends and relatives are unlikely to serve as effective mentors. They don't want to hurt your feelings (except for those who might, for various reasons, be eager to take a swipe at your ego). If you're fortunate, you'll know somebody—ideally a professional writer who is also a careful reader and astute editor—with whom you can exchange criticism. If you don't have a mentor, consider paying somebody to criticize your work. It's better to hear criticism from a mentor at this stage, when you can do something about it, than to be rejected by a publisher.

John Irving has said, "It's my experience that very few writers, young or old, are really seeking advice when they give out their work to be read. They want support; they want someone to say, 'Good job.'"

It's *my* experience that those "very few" writers who really do seek advice are the ones who are most likely to succeed. A pat on the back and a hearty "Good job" are not very helpful.

Mentors often see flaws that you can't see because you are too close to your story. Don't automatically and uncritically change everything your mentor finds fault with. But consider all the suggestions and criticisms.

The last word

Now your story is finished. It is, you honestly believe, the best you can possibly make it. You've nurtured it and fought with it, cried with it and laughed at it. It's time to make the final copy and send it off.

It can be a scary time. Erica Jong once admitted, "I went for years not finishing anything. Because, of course, when you finish something you can be judged."

Those living characters, that clever puzzle with all its neat clues, all those vivid places and dramatic events and significant themes that have occupied your consciousness for a year or more—all are abruptly gone. "Writing a book," said Daphne Du Maurier, "is like a purge; at the end of it one is empty . . . like a dry shell on the beach, waiting for the tide to come in again."

Sending off a manuscript can leave you feeling empty. The only cure is to start writing something else. And if your story or novel fails to sell, keep writing anyway. Writers write. Many successful authors have trunks full of early manuscripts they could not—or didn't even try to—sell. If they'd allowed their early failures to discourage them, they never would have kept at it.

Writing is a non-stop learning process. Write regularly and write often. Practice your craft. The more you write, the better you'll become. And when you hold that first copy of your own book in your hand, you'll know that it's been worth every agonizing moment.